NEW AGE OR OLD LIE?

New Age or Old Lie?

KERRY D. McROBERTS

HENDRICKSON PUBLISHERS
PEABODY, MASSACHUSETTS 01961-3473

140064

Copyright © 1989
Hendrickson Publishers, Inc.
P.O. Box 3473
Peabody, Massachusetts 01961–3473

ISBN 0–943575–30–3

Second printing — December, 1992

Library of Congress Cataloging-in-Publication Data

McRoberts, Kerry.
    New age or old lie? / Kerry McRoberts.
        p.   cm.
    ISBN 0–943575–30–3
    1. New Age movement–Controversial literature.
2. Apologetics–20th century.   I. Title.
BP605.N48M388 1989
299'.93–dc20   89–12831
                                                            CIP

To my wife, Vicki,
a faithful companion and unfailing
Christian servant for whom I am grateful.

and

SPECIAL DEDICATION
in memory of
DR. WALTER R. MARTIN

The late Dr. Walter R. Martin was both a mentor and a friend
whose influence upon my life and ministry are inestimable. It is my
extreme privilege to dedicate this book to his memory. People throughout the world were impacted by Dr. Martin's boldness and unashamed
commitment to the Cross of Christ. Dr. Martin was a humble and caring
individual who loved people so much that he was unwilling to com-
promise truth, as revealed in Holy Scripture. Few have contributed so
much to the kingdom of God.

Table of Contents

Foreword

Kerry McRoberts has given us a carefully written, scholarly analysis of one of the most discussed socio-religious movements of our day. The intrusion of New Age thinking in our culture is increasingly evident in every major thread of our social fabric. New Age influence can be found in science, education, the health professions, entertainment, business, and even the military. Its impact on individuals as well as groups can be seen in the following random illustrations:

— A network of Seattle architects, artists, and dowsers calling themselves the Geo Group have identified forty-four "power centers" in that city which they claim have the capability of affecting consciousness as well as storing emotions and feelings much like a battery retains energy. They hope to identify various forms of Earth energies and to cooperate with the "Earth Spirit" to improve the flow of these energies. Their New Age public artworks project was funded by the Seattle Arts Commission.

— An article in the *Los Angeles Times* describes an Oregon conference of political activists associated with the ecology-oriented "Green movement" in which participants "formed a circle under a blue night sky to sing and pound drums and chant quasi-pagan hymns to Mother Earth." Conferees were reminded of recent dramatic gains made by various "Green" political parties in Europe.

— A New Age church advertises a unique four-hour seminar, "Transformation Through Fire," which promises to teach people how to turn their fear and limitations into power and success by learning how to walk unharmed on burning coals. The seminar claims to provide participants with a "lasting power to create richer, fuller, and more productive lives, and an ability to integrate the spiritual realm into daily experience." The seminar was held in one of America's most affluent suburbs. The registration fee for this exercise in spiritual awareness? Eighty dollars.

— Verna Yater, director of the California-based Spiritual Sciences Institute, reports that over 10,000 seekers have come to her since 1978 to experience channeling, the term currently used to describe mediumship. She claims that such encounters represent "an opportunity for people to have a non-dogmatic spiritual experience." While the sessions may be non-dogmatic, they aren't cheap. Yater charges $125 per hour to bring forth "healing sounds from the angelic realms."

— The U. S. Army negotiated a one-year, $350,000 contract with "Sportsmind"–a program for improving athletic performance developed by New Age entrepreneur Chris Majer–to train Green Berets. According to *Command* magazine, soldiers were taught how to visualize combat tasks and how to meditate in order to better hide out behind enemy lines.

These are just a few examples of how the New Age has entered the mainstream of American life. It is inaccurate to assume that New Agers are unstable, irrational, residual hippies living at the margins of society. Research has demonstrated that those persons most likely to embrace New Age thinking and practices tend to be educated, affluent, and successful people. They must be taken seriously. This is what Kerry McRoberts does in the book you hold in your hands. He does not focus on the sensational and bizarre aspects of the New Age movement. He reminds us that New Age mysticism is more than the latest fad in crystals and has more staying power than Shirley MacLaine's books.

The author does not assume a reactionary stance toward the material he discusses, a strategy that other Christian observers have not always adopted. Instead, he carefully traces the roots of the New Age appeal and then demonstrates the reasonableness of the Christian faith. At the heart of his apologetic is the focal importance of the resurrection of Jesus Christ.

What I find so refreshing about this book is the fact that while the author presents a well-documented analysis of the alternative altars of the New Age, he reiterates so convincingly the total adequacy and relevance of the Christian faith for those who seek personal and planetary transformation.

It has always been my conviction that the primary task of the church is to proclaim the gospel. This book will help any serious reader to accomplish that goal, especially as we attempt to make clear the truth claims of the gospel to those who have been deceived by a lie as old as human history.

Ronald Enroth
Westmont College
Santa Barbara, California
June 1989

Preface

The New Age is a plethora of disparate organizations and individuals polarized around pseudo-scientific, psychospiritual, and mythic themes. The cosmopolitan spirit of the New Age has touched every facet of Western civilization, including science, medicine, education, business, social sciences, religion, politics, and sports.

America's pluralism has provided the New Age a stage for its positive message of hope through human transformation. Pluralism has created a spiritual-ideological vacuum within our troubled civilization. The New Age has the potential and is gaining the momentum necessary to effectively fill our spiritually vacuous society with its ideology and values.

The New Age presents a great challenge to the Christian Church. However, merely because the New Age agenda involves the incorporation of an ominous world system, this does not mean that the Church should react with paranoia. The Church has been confronted with evil from its inception, as both Scripture and history demonstrate. Therefore, rather than a sensationalized reaction, often based upon unsubstantiated speculations about prophetic fulfillment and hidden dangers, we need to address rationally the New Age and our culture with biblical conviction and wisdom.

This book is more than merely an exposé of the New Age Movement; it is a defense of the Christian faith as an integral and necessary part of presenting the gospel of Jesus Christ to our contemporary culture. The uniqueness of this book, among many already written on the subject, is its demonstration that Christianity is not obsolete, as New Agers would have our culture believe. Founded upon the resurrection of Jesus Christ, Christianity remains the only hope of all mankind.

My research into the New Age Movement began in Southern California as a student at the Simon Greenleaf School of Law. As a part of the requirements for the Master of Arts degree in Christian apologetics, I wrote my thesis on the subject of the New Age Movement. My thesis advisor was Dr. Walter R. Martin, apologist extraordinaire. My indebtedness to Dr. Martin and the Christian Research Institute is obvious throughout this book.

Acknowledgments

There are numerous people to whom I wish to express my deepest gratitude for their help and encouragement during the researching and writing of this book. My expression of gratitude does not make any of these individuals responsible for the views and shortcomings of this book, for which I take full responsibility.

Hendrickson Publishers, especially Dave Townsley and Patrick Alexander, has been patient and gracious in helping a new author. Kin Millen is a professional and a true friend for whom I am very thankful. The faculty and administration, especially Dr. D. V. Hurst and Marshall Flowers, of Northwest College are greatly appreciated. Dr. Walter R. Martin was both a mentor and an inspiration to my life and ministry. The Christian Research Institute and the Spiritual Counterfeits Project have contributed much to my understanding of the New Age and cultic/occultic trends. Dr. Harold Lindsell, a fearless contender for biblical integrity, and Dr. J. I. Packer of Regent College are a constant encouragement to me by their Christ-like examples. I wish to thank members of Sumner Assembly of God for their unselfish support and love for their pastor. A special thanks to my board of deacons and my secretary, Lori Fogaras. Thanks is to be extended as well to Deanna Osburn, a faithful Christian friend. My father, John H. McRoberts, and brother, Jay McRoberts, deserve special recognition. Finally, my wife, Vicki, and daughters, Kari and Traci, who have paid a great price for this book, are appreciated and loved above all.

Kerry D. McRoberts
Sumner, Washington
April 1989

1 | A New Age?

"Love what you are. Love the god that you are. Embrace the wind, and the willow, and the water, for it is the creation of your importance, and be at peace," says Ramtha, a 35,000 year-old warrior spirit which speaks through an attractive, lithe blonde from Yelm, Washington.[1] J. Z. Knight is known as a channeler for Ramtha, who once conquered the mythical kingdom of occult lore, Atlantis, and has now returned to the earthly plane to give spiritual guidance to literally thousands of people in America seeking entrance into a New Age. "The Ram" (as Ramtha is affectionately called), whose clientele includes actresses Shirley MacLaine and Linda Evans, predicts that the New Age will dawn in the year 2000.

Ramtha is only one among a myriad of "spirit guides" which are preparing the consciousness of individuals to enter into an age of universal enlightenment. "You need answers," says a harsh guttural voice through the clench-fisted, entranced channeler. "I am here to answer you."[2]

The controversial claims of Ramtha and a host of others (human and non-human!) who predict a coming New Age of planetary paradise for the inhabitants of earth was the focus of an open forum I recently participated in at Seattle Pacific University. Eight panel members, four representing Evangelical Christianity and four representing New Age thought, individually responded to the primary issue of the evening, what is the New Age Movement?

Responses to this question were varied: "it is a mystical, mind-altering experience. . . . it is contrary to a Judeo-Christian world view."

A New Ager countered, "The New Age Movement says that the source of God is the source of love and the source of God is within you; . . . this was Jesus' message." Another advocate of the New Age added, "The New Age is an age where new perceptions enable us to explore the unknown frontiers of our universe." A representative of Evangelical Christianity contentiously replied, "for the first time in history there is a viable movement, the New Age Movement, that truly meets all the scriptural requirements for the Antichrist." "The New Age," retorted a somewhat indignant New Ager, "is typified by the individual's search to understand his own relationship to the God-force . . . the Christ within." The sincere commitment of the New Age to planetary survival was pleaded for by yet another "Aquarian conspirator." "The New Age is one of the most creative movements in the last part of the twentieth century. . . . The attempt of the New Age . . . is to understand and be energized to meet the crises that are facing us today."

The diversity of the New Age has been analogized by one writer to the "proverbial elephant discovered independently by three blind men: one came upon his leg, and likened him as a tree; another got hold of his trunk and likened him to a hose; the third stumbled upon his tail and insisted he was like a rope."[3] This illustrates an invaluable point: when critiquing the New Age, we need to be aware that the consensus of a part may not be true of the whole.

The New Age is not simply another new cult, but an emerging world view, a new way of thinking that is being subtly introduced to multitudes in Western civilization. This new way of thinking promises renewed hope to those disillusioned with former inadequate world views such as atheistic humanism. Through a change of consciousness (transformation in New Age terminology) the New Age seeks to bring about radical changes within the world community that will deliver the earth from its present sociopolitical ills.

The New Age is an extremely large, loosely structured network of organizations and individuals. The New Age weds the humanism of the West with the spirituality of Eastern occult mysticism. The union of these two unlikely bedfellows inflates former concepts of human potential in the West to unlimited proportions, generating a belief in the deification of man.

Several cults emphasizing a mystical experience (e.g., Transcendental Meditation, Church Universal and Triumphant, the Divine Light Mission, Scientology, Eckankar) subscribe to the New Age world view.

Various organizations and cults that are a part of the "human potential movement" also share this world view. Familiar groups included here are est (Erhard Seminars Training, also referred to as Forum), Lifespring, Silva Mind Control, the Esalen Institute, and Summit Workshops. A significant number (though not all) of the holistic health centers in America also promote the New Age way of thinking. Individual followers of gurus (Baba Ram Dass, Sai Baba, Da Free John, etc.), agnostics, atheists, theologically liberal "Christians," and secularists in general all have representation in the ranks of New Age ideology.

Although there is a wide range of beliefs and emphases among groups and individuals that come under the collective banner of the New Age Movement, certain basic assumptions are true of the whole. The edifice of New Age thought rests upon five distinctive philosophical pillars.

1. Reality Is a "Seamless Garment"

New Age thinking embraces the concept that everything in existence is one essential reality. The universe is perceived as a "seamless garment" without distinctions; all that is, is one reality.

Monism is another name for a "seamless," undifferentiated universe. Monism is a concept of Vedic Hinduism. Monos (Greek) means single; and therefore, ultimate reality is a single, organic whole without independent parts. Only reality wears the seamless garment, everything else is naked illusion.

Although the New Age embraces monism, it does not believe, as classic Vedic Hinduism, that the world is illusory or maya. The New Age is more of "a Western expression of monism."[4] Holding to its Western heritage, the New Age is world affirming. In other words, the external world is really there. It is not an illusion. The New Age has a paradoxical view of reality. Objects, events, and persons maintain a distinctiveness, and yet they are interdependent with the whole, a part of one flowing reality. As the offspring of two convergent world views, the New Age Movement has characteristics of both parents.

Eastern monism suffers from grave epistemological (in philosophy, the grounds for knowledge) uncertainty. Monism is fatalistic in its view of the need to reject personality in order to attain to one's spiritual awareness (enlightenment). This results in an inescapable tension between the logic of what it teaches and the logic of who and what man really is. Eastern monism, therefore, fails to provide a sufficient spiritual option for Western man, who is faced with the dehumanizing influences of the failing world view of atheistic humanism.

Atheistic humanism views man as the product of primordial, non-intelligent mass that by mere chance alone evolved to a human state of existence. Therefore, man is nothing more than a cosmic accident who has no inherent purpose. No matter how sublime our descriptions of man, this view ultimately strips man of any intrinsic self-worth. Since New Age man envisions himself on the threshold of a golden era, he must stretch his imagination beyond rational boundaries to embrace Eastern monism and Western humanism as legitimate means of saving humanity from apocalyptic catastrophe.

2. God Wears the "Seamless Garment"

The belief that God is all in all, or that all that exists is an extension of God's essence, is pantheism. Apart from God, there is no true reality. Pantheism imbues the material universe with consciousness. Therefore, according New Age thinking, matter is not dead, as in the thinking of the naturalist; instead, an impersonal force or consciousness is the essence of all reality. The "Force" of Star Wars fits into this type of metaphysical mode.

G. K. Chesterton poignantly observed that, "when a man ceases to believe in God, he does not believe in nothing. He believes in anything." Rather than a step of evolutionary progress, pantheism is a regression into pagan idolatry. Pantheism is the attitude into which the human mind will automatically fall when left to itself. Pantheism is what man says about God, instead of what God says about man. It is therefore not surprising that we, as sinful humans, find pantheism so congenial.

Ludwig Wittgenstein correctly stated (*Tractatus Logico-Philosophicus*): "If there is any value that does have value, it must lie outside the whole sphere of what happens and is the case. . . . Ethics is transcendental." Pantheism, however, fails to provide an unchanging, transcendent point of reference for ethical decisions. If all that exists is one undifferentiated whole, then categories of good and evil are ultimately abandoned. Men are left with the inability to distinguish right from wrong in this kind of universe.

Men quite obviously are unable to live this way. Men must make ethical distinctions between good and evil, right and wrong. Norman Geisler observes that "In order to discover if a man really believes it is good to be just, do not look at the way he acts toward others; rather, look at the way he reacts when others do something to him."[5] Pantheism is self-defeating with regard to practical human experience.

3. Man Wears the "Seamless Garment"

It follows from pantheism that if God is all and all is God, then man, as a part of the "all," must be inherently god.

In the late sixties, during my undergraduate days at the University of Oregon, a question concerning ultimate reality was circulating around campus: "How are you going to recognize God when you get to heaven?" The reply: "By the big *G* on his sweatshirt."

The New Age, however, boldly declares that man really wears the sweatshirt with the big *G*. "Each of us," claims David Spangler, "is a dynamic process of God revealing himself."[6] Singer John Denver, a graduate of Erhard Seminars Training (Forum), enthusiastically agrees, "I can do anything. One of these days, I'll be so complete I won't be a human, I'll be a god."[7]

Beginning with evolutionary presuppositions as an explanation for the material existence of the universe, the New Age man sees himself at the peak of his evolutionary cycle. The birth of a mystical humanism is viewed as the result of an evolutionary metamorphosis wherein the New Age man has attained to godhood. New Age man, attired in his "sweatshirt," fearlessly kicks open the door of the occult, announcing his unqualified divinity.

Occult philosophy is the flip-side of secular humanism. The occult, like humanism, stresses human potential through its exalted view of man as the source of all meaning in the universe. The occult, however, inflates human potential to cosmic dimensions and thereby deifies humanity. Occult philosophy defines God in terms of being created in the image of man. The occult phenomenon in America is the logical conclusion to a world view that insists upon the absolute autonomy of man.

The Pseudo-scientific Terminology of the Occult

Because of the use of scientific or pseudo-scientific labels, occult practices (i.e., yoga, visualization, spiritism, witchcraft, etc.) within the New Age go unnoticed. The deceptive packaging of the New Age grows out of a deliberate design of the occult to adapt itself to the prevailing cultural environment. Transcendental Meditation's venerated guru, Maharishi Mahesh Yogi, explains:

> If the message is to be carried from generation to generation, it should be placed on the mass tendency of each generation. . . . Therefore, basically, the teaching . . . should be based on that phase of life which at a particular time is guiding the destiny of mass consciousness. . . . Thus the proper plan for the emancipation of all mankind, generation after generation, lies in . . . finding various ways and means for its propagation according to the consciousness of the times.[8]

The Maharishi is saying that the religious goals of his movement should not be presented in terms that are popular and acceptable to the majority of people. In chameleonlike fashion, the occult adapts its terminology to the vernacular of the social milieu it is attempting to influence; yet the meaning behind the artificial term is quite different from what people initially conceive.

> Whenever . . . religion dominates the mass consciousness, Transcendental . . . meditation should be taught in terms of religion. Whenever metaphysical thinking dominates . . . [it] should be taught in metaphysical terms, openly aiming at the fulfillment of the current metaphysical thought. Whenever . . . politics dominates . . . [it] should be taught in terms of and from the platform of politics, aiming at bringing fulfillment to the political aspirations of the generation.[9]

The psycho-occult philosophy of the human potential movement is wrapped in scientific and therapeutic terminology. The saffron robes, shaved heads, and incense are replaced with three-piece suits, pseudo-scientific technology, and an emphasis on human potential.

The "Inner Truth" of the Occult

Inherent within the nature of the occult is the concept of an "inner truth" (the real truth known only to occult initiates) and an "outer truth" (the attractive, yet misleading face presented to the public). The successful penetration of the New Age into Western culture is due, in large part, to the deceptive design of a gap between an "inner truth" and an "outer truth." The vibrantly positive facade of the New Age acts as "sheep's clothing" for the spiritual delusion of the occult.

4. Cosmic Consciousness

Ultimate reality is a "seamless garment." God wears the "seamless garment." To the Western mindset, such a spiritual orientation appears rather insipid for its lack of diversity. What seems to be the problem? Ignorance. Timothy Leary of sixties infamy puts it this way:

> Our favorite concepts are standing in the way of a flood tide two billion years building up. The verbal dam is collapsing. Head for the hills or prepare your intellectual craft to flow with the current.[10]

We need to abandon the psychological limitations of Western thought and turn East. Man needs a change of consciousness, a mystical experience, to be made aware that he is really wearing the sweatshirt with the big *G* on the front, argues the New Age.

"Mystical states," says William James, "seem to those who experience them to be states of knowledge. They are insights into depths of truth unplumbed by the discursive intellect."[11] New Age author Marilyn Ferguson goes beyond a mere description of cosmic consciousness to the experience itself:

> Loss of ego boundaries and the sudden identification with all of life (a melting into the universe); lights; altered color perception; thrills; electrical sensations; sense of expanding like a bubble or bounding upward; banishment of force, particularly fear of death; soaring sound; wind; feeling of being separated from physical self; bliss; sharp awareness of patterns; a sense of liberation; a blending of the senses (synesthesia), as when colors are heard and sights produce and auditory sensations; an oceanic feeling; a belief that one has awakened; that the experience is the only reality and that ordinary consciousness is but its poor shadow; and a sense of transcending time and space.[12]

Direct mystical states are the norm in the New Age. Propositional revelation (such as the Bible) is considered to be a barrier to spiritual awareness. Experience is the final authority. Methodology is deemphasized. Therefore, numerous mystical-inducing methods are practiced by adherents of the New Age Movement in order to attain cosmic consciousness. Techniques include Eastern meditation, yoga, martial arts, visualization, guided imagery, hypnosis, biofeedback, body therapies (rolfing, bioenergetics, kinesiology), seminar training (Erhard Seminar Training, Silva Mind Control, Foundation for Mind Research, Arica Institute), sensitivity groups, and many others.

In the New Age, the expanded consciousness of man is believed to be the most powerful acting force on the physical plane. The energies required in the ethereal counterpart to bring in the New Age are occultly under the control of human consciousness. The reordering of reality is limited to man's own state of mind, for the "New Age is consciousness first, form later."[13]

> Man must learn to build that culture through his atunement to the ideas of New Age, to externalize its characteristics from within his own creative consciousness. In this he will find his new glory and his fulfillment as a builder of a new heaven and a new earth.[14]

As the New Age man attunes his consciousness with the consciousness of ultimate reality, the idea of the New Age will materialize on earth.

Chris Griscom is a channeler from New Mexico. To her, the idealism of the New Age means, "We are the stars of our own movie. . . . We are writing the script at all times."[15] In his book, *The Center of the Cyclone*, John Lilly is exuberant about reaching "+3," the highest state of consciousness:

> We are creating energy, matter and life at the interface between the void and all known creation. We are facing into the known universe, creating it, filling it. . . . I am "one of the boys in the engine room pumping creation from the void in the known universe; from the unknown to the known I am pumping."[16]

For sociologist George Leonard, altered states of consciousness have brought him to the realization that "I am the universe."[17] In the New Age, the search for the higher self is united with the search for ultimate reality.

Channeling

Mafu is a "spirit guide" like Ramtha. Mafu is channeled by Penny Torres of Southern California. Mafu informs his audience that he has passed through four dimensions and 1908 years to bring his enlightening news to the inhabitants of earth: "I am an enlightened entity and I come to you from the Brotherhood of light."[18] Mafu claims that former President Ronald Reagan discussed a better day for the people of earth with "peoples of the inner earth." These "people" supposedly gain access to the Oval Office through secret polar tunnels![19]

Jach Pursel, a former insurance adjuster, is the channel for Lazaris. Lazaris, speaking with a British accent and a slight lisp, describes himself as "the consummate friend." The round, bearded Pursel sits on a simple platform in front of 400 people at Los Angeles's Hilton Hotel for a weekend seminar. Among Lazaris's guests is actress Sharon Gless, the feisty blonde detective of *Cagney and Lacy*. Gless sobs along with several others as Lazaris's comforting tones guide the crowd into the metaphysical wonderland of the New Age magic kingdom. The wounded psyches of those in attendance are placed in the hands of their trusted therapist, Lazaris. Soon it is time to leave the ethereal fantasyland and return to the physical plane. The reentry is made easier by Lazaris's assurances that, "You are now healed mentally; your old patterns can now be said no to."[20]

Kevin Ryerson is a colorful channeler. Ryerson is unique among New Age channelers in that he is a medium for five spirit entities, not just one. Among the disembodied residents of Ryerson's corporeal habitat are "John," an Essene scholar from the first century A.D., and an Irish pickpocket from the Elizabethan era known as "Tom MacPherson." Ryerson's fascination with the paranormal goes back to his childhood: "When all other kids were putting together model airplanes, I was studying ESP and Zener cards."[21] Influenced by Edgar Cayce (Cayce, who died in 1945, was a famous psychic known for his diagnosis of medical problems while in a trance), Ryerson is working with Dr. William Kautz of the Center for Applied Intuition in San Francisco in an effort to bring resolution to scientific mysteries.

Perhaps weekend seminars with average price tags of between $250 to $400 or private sessions priced at $90–$150 an hour are a little steep for many people. There are a number of cut-rate personal channelers available for those who either can't or just don't want to afford the more costly vintages of metaphysical insights served by Ramtha, Mafu, Lazaris, or John.

Harvey Huggins is a retired logger who lives in Oregon. For the meager price of a can of Copenhagen smokeless tobacco, Huggins will turn over his vocal cords to Wishpoosh, the beaver warrior-god of the Chinook Indians. The price of admission is worth it just to see how

Huggins comes into contact with his entity. Huggins plunges his head into a bucket of water for a few minutes. As the old logger emerges and shakes the water from his beard, Wishpoosh is ready to share his metaphysical quips with the adventuresome.

If Nebraska is more convenient to the seeker of low-budget cosmic wisdom, then Cyril Jones is available. Jones channels the crass Mac-Doogie, a Scottish Highlander and warrior-accountant who lived in 23 B.C. MacDoogie hasn't changed in all these centuries of time; he'll tell you anything you want to know for a fifth of Glenlivet.

Roger Dodger is from Maine. Ramjet must find himself in comfortable surroundings living inside of Roger in Maine, for he is also from the high country—Tibet to be exact. Ramjet was a Shao Lin warrior-monk who lived around A.D. 900. You would think that a consultation with such an impressive figure as Ramjet would cost at least as much as Ramtha. Not so! Roger Dodger owns a gas station in Pidwick, Maine, and the insightful consultations of Ramjet, the "one who lubricates the Wheel of Karma," are available to all customers. Just come in and fill 'er up!

Are these entities real? Are their channels for real? There are at least three possible responses to these questions. First of all, the entities are a part of the channeler's higher consciousness, and the message is sincere. Second, the entity is an actual spiritual being; and in the third case, the channeler is a fraud, feigning possession for the purpose of financial gain.

When interpreting messages "from the other side," their moral-theological content must be judged. The messages of the channelers are generally amoral, self-centered, paganistic affirmations of man's sinlessness and inherent godhood. Brooks Alexander further comments that "The thrust of most spirit messages is to deny the reality of death and its function as judgment. The Bible implies that judgment is a spur to conscience, which convicts us of sin and leads us to our need of repentance and redemption."[22]

Reincarnation

What if an individual fails to recognize his inherent divinity? For many New Agers, reincarnation is the answer to this psychic dilemma. Reincarnationists believe that the soul experiences multiple lives, gradually attaining a state of perfection in which oneness with the impersonal God of pantheism is realized.[23] Actress Shirley MacLaine recalls numerous past lives. MacLaine believes she once lived as "a young Buddhist monk, an orphan child adopted by a herd of elephants, a Colonial settler . . . during the signing of the U.S. Constitution, a ballet dancer in Russia and a Mongolian maid raped by a bandit."[24]

Intrinsic to Eastern spirituality, regardless of the appearance of ethics or the sophisticated-sounding philosophy, is open idolatry, animism, and spiritism. New Age spirituality is non-historical and non-revelational. Experience alone becomes the norm by which to test spiritual realities. The New Age mystic is left with an irrational form of spirituality based on a religious experience. For the New Age, the appeal of raw spiritual power squelches any concern to evaluate its legitimacy. Few bother to inquire after the source of spiritual expression.

5. All Religions Are Equal Roads to God

Typical of New Age gurus is to paint all of the religions of the world with the same pantheistic brush. The claim of equality among religions and the belief that they ultimately, at their core, really teach the same thing is syncretism. Benjamin Creme, an "esotericist" and New Age spokesman, states:

> Throughout history, humanity's evolution has been guided by a group of enlightened men, the Masters of Wisdom. They have remained largely in the remote desert and mountain places of earth, working mainly through disciples who live openly in the world. The message of the Christ's reappearance has been given primarily by such a disciple, trained for his task for over 20 years. At the center of this "spiritual Hierarchy" stands the World Teacher, Lord Maitreya, known by Christians as the Christ. And as Christians await the Second Coming, so the Jews await the Messiah, the Buddhists the fifth Buddha, the Moslems the Imam Mahdi, and the Hindus await Krishna. These are all names for one individual. His presence in the world guarantees there will be no third World War.[25]

Some parallels can be drawn among the religions of the world relative to their historical development and existing ethical standards; however, basic doctrinal tenets stand in great contrast among the religions of the world.

Contrary to former notions of the evolution of religion, some anthropologists and archaeologists suggest that monotheism (the worship of one God) is the most ancient form of religious worship.[26] Among primitive religions, the one God has been replaced with many gods (polytheism) who eventually withdraw so far from man that they become inactive in the religious life of man. The gods are seen as disinheriting their earthly involvement to a son or a demiurge whose mission is to finish or perfect creation. Gradually religious practice degenerates further to the worship of mythical ancestors, mother-goddesses, the fecundating gods, and the like.[27] The evidence indicates a degeneracy from a true knowledge and worship of the one God.

The above-mentioned observations serve to demonstrate the religious schizophrenia that characterizes the syncretism of the New Age Movement. This can be shown by the following illustration:

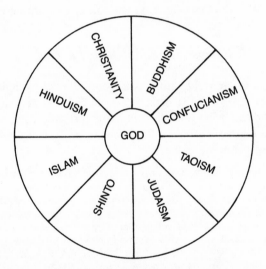

This circle graph represents the major religions of the world. Each of the major religions of the world claims to teach us something about ultimate reality and the relationship of man to that ultimate reality (God, cosmos, etc.). Inductively, we can eliminate many of the world's religions as legitimate because of their failure to conform to the evidence supporting monotheism. Buddhism is agnostic (philosophical view that insists we cannot know that there is a God). Confucianism is likewise agnostic. Hinduism is polytheistic. Taoism is characterized by metaphysical dualism. Metaphysical dualism is the religious concept of two eternal, impersonal forces; one is positive (Yang) and one is negative (Yin). The impersonal forces of Yang and Yin represent a degeneracy from, not a conformity to, monotheistic religion. Shintoism is henotheistic. Henotheism is the worship of one supreme or local deity. Henotheism acknowledges the existence of many gods in common with polytheism.

Islam is one of the three remaining monotheistic religions. However, Islam derives from both Judaism and Christianity. It follows then, that the newer "revelation" (the Koran) must conform to the older revelation (the Bible) in order to validate its truth claims. The God of the Bible (Yahweh) never changes because of his eternal nature (Malachi 3:6). It is irrational to conclude, therefore, that God would communicate something to one generation and then centuries later communicate something entirely different to another generation. Islam, however, makes such false claims.[28]

Finally, we come to Judaism and Christianity. Christianity is indebted to Judaism. Christianity inherited four fundamental concepts from Judaism:

(1) Monotheistic worship
(2) The personhood of God
(3) The concept of verbal revelation (the Bible)
(4) The idea that God intervenes in real, space-time human history.[29]

The Messiah is also from Jewish lineage. In the person of Jesus Christ, it can be demonstrated that Christianity is the fulfillment of the Mosaic Law and the Jewish prophets.[30]

The New Age disregards both history and basic doctrinal tenets in its efforts to syncretize the religions of the world. However, Christianity "is the only religion which purports to offer external, objective evidence of its validity. All other religions appeal to inner experience without any means of objective validation."[31]

The Christ of the New Age

David Spangler speaks of Christ in pagan-pantheistic terms:

However, the Cosmic Christ did not come only for humanity, but in service to all evolving life streams of all the kingdoms of Nature upon

the planet. Through the channel made for him by the human consciousness of Jesus, the Christ entered the very structure and life of Earth and
united with his counterpart within the Earth Logos.[32]

Mark and Elizabeth Clare Prophet of the Church Universal and
Triumphant are also representative of New Age thought's denial of the
person of Jesus as Christ:

> The Master's greatest desire was that they should not mistake the son
> of Man (Jesus) for the Son of God (the Christ). Should confusion arise
> regarding the source of his humanity (in Christ) and the source of his
> divinity (in God), the Savior knew that generations to come would not
> worship the Christ, but the man Jesus.[33]

Benjamin Creme states that Jesus is divine "in exactly the sense
that we are divine."[34] Speaking of Jesus, Creme further asserts that "He
is Divine, having perfected Himself and manifested the Divinity potential in each of us."[35] Shirley MacLaine goes way out on a limb in her
proclamation concerning the Son of God: "Christ was the most advanced human ever to walk on this planet."[36]

Many pantheists deny that Jesus died on the Cross: "Jesus did
not sleep within the tomb."[37] Levi Dowling describes the resurrection
of Jesus Christ in the occult tradition as a transmutation from "carnal
flesh and blood to flesh of God."[38]

Occultists believe that Jesus went through degrees of initiation
which are open to all men. Upon entering the world, Jesus was a third-
degree "initiate." He became a fourth-degree "initiate" at his crucifixion and a fifth-degree "initiate" after his resurrection.

The Jesus of the Bible did not come into the world to show us
that he was like God but rather to reveal to man that God was like
him (John 1:18). Jesus Christ is the fullness of the Godhead in human
flesh (Colossians 2:9). Therefore, Jesus is not merely an illuminated man,
he is the incarnation of the living God (John 1:1; 1:14). Chapter six
of this book will provide a refutation of New Age perversions concerning Jesus Christ as a part of an apologetic for his bodily resurrection
from the dead.

Connections/Networking/General Systems Theory

"Connections" is a New Age concept of the interconnectedness
of all of the separate components in existence.[39] A university professor

describes this concept as "a kind of magical circle, an unbroken unity with all life and cosmic processes, including my own life."[40]

Connections are intrinsic to New Age ideology. Connections are revered as the basis for the New Age perspective of holism. The ultimate expression of holism in the New Age is one unified sociopolitical world system. Marilyn Ferguson further explains:

> Because these connections can only be sustained by a flow of energy, the system is always in flux. Notice the paradox; the more coherent or intricately connected the structure, the more unstable it is. Increased coherence means increased instability! This very instability is the key to transformation. The dissipation of energy, as Prigogine demonstrated by his elegant mathematics, creates the potential for sudden reordering.[41]

A "sudden reordering" refers to the spiritual transformation of the earth resulting in the emergence of the New Age.

Connections provide a modem for "Networks." Jessica Lipnack and Jeffrey Stamps, coauthors of *Networking*, inform us that:

> Networks are composed of self-reliant and autonomous participants— people and organizations who simultaneously function as independent "wholes" and as interdependent "parts."[42]

Networking is like casting a net over the multitude of organizations and individuals within the New Age, interconnecting them for the purpose of information distribution.

Teilhard de Chardin, a patron saint among New Agers, believed in an expanding layer of consciousness that permeated the "noosphere." Chardin spoke of his noosphere as becoming a cultural reality: "Like the meridians as they approach the poles, science, philosophy and religion are bound to converge as they draw nearer to the whole."[43] Networks are seen as the reality of Chardin's dreams.

Networks shun bureaucratic or hierarchical configurations, emphasizing rather a decentralization of power in accomplishing global transformation.

> Just as a bureaucracy is less than the sum of its parts, a network is many times greater than the sum of its parts. This is a source of power never before tapped in history. Multiple self-sufficient social movements linked for a whole array of goals whose accomplishment would transform every aspect of contemporary life.[44]

Networks bring "like-minded" people together by "conferences, phone calls, air travel, books, phantom organizations, papers, pamphleteering, photocopying, lectures, workshops, parties, grapevines, mutual friends, summit meetings, coalitions, tapes, newsletters."[45] Because of an emphasis upon a decentralization of power there are "tens of thousands of entry points" into the web of networks that are intertwined throughout the multifaceted New Age Movement.[46]

General Systems Theory is a related concept to networks. General Systems Theory presupposes the indivisible unity of the universe (monism). Every separate variable of any system is united with other variables like the links of a chain. Cause and effect are indistinguishable, according to this theory, because all variables are essentially one unified whole. This theory forms the basis for relationships, a sacred value in New Age thought.

The author of General Systems Theory, Ludwig von Bertalanffy, explains his view of all things in existence as one organic whole:

> Its applications range from the biophysics of cellular processes to the dynamics of populations, from the problems of physics to those of psychiatry and those of political and cultural units.

> General Systems Theory is symptomatic of a change in our world view. No longer do we see the world in a blind play of atoms, but rather a great organization.[47]

Syntropy (the Greek prefix *syn* means "together with") is a term applied in New Age ideology to the increasing organization of relationships within the systems of the universe. This concept is critical to the New Age value of the interconnectedness of all components within the universe.

A Paradigm Shift

In order for a new planetary culture to emerge, New Agers insist that we must first experience a paradigm shift. A paradigm is a conceptual model used for the interpretation of human experience. The transformation that the New Age seeks is the orientation of humanity to its own world view (paradigm) and brand of spirituality.

Physicist Fritjof Capra is among many intellectuals who see modern man as the vanguard of the new world order. Capra points to numerous global crises in order to stress the need for a transformation of consciousness among humanity:

More than fifteen million people—most of them children—die of starvation each year; another 500 million are seriously undernourished. Almost 40 percent of the world's population has no access to professional health services; yet developing countries spend more than three times as much on armaments as on health care. Thirty-five percent of humanity lacks safe drinking water, while half of its scientists and engineers are engaged in the technology of making weapons.[48]

Modern man is incapable of dealing with complex social ills such as inflation, psychoses, disease, famine, and crime. Capra uses this as evidence to indict former ways of thinking, stressing that they are obsolete. Modern man needs new modes of thought in order to capably address and resolve the problems of today's world. Marilyn Ferguson agrees with Capra:

> We try to solve problems with our existing tools, in their old context, instead of seeing that the escalating crisis is a symptom of our essential wrongheadedness.[49]

As the minds of humanity are transformed and, "When the moon is in the seventh house, and Jupiter aligns with Mars; then peace will guide the planets, and love will steer the stars."[50] This, according to New Agers, will climax in the birth of the New Age, a planetary paradise.

The conception and birth of this new world view can be more fully understood by examining the historical process of Western man's exaltation and final rejection of reason. The escape from reason has resulted in modern man's unrestrained acceptance of occult mysticism. Chapter two will summarize Western thought from the Enlightenment to the present to explain why this modern occult is experiencing a resurgence in Western civilization.

A COMPARISON OF WORLD VIEWS

	New Age World View	Biblical World View
Reality	The Universe is one essential, undifferentiated whole (Monism). Unlike Hinduism the material world does exist. However, it is a transmaterial universe.	God created the universe and all things within it (including man) from nothing (ex nihilo; Genesis 1; Isaiah 45:18–19). All things were created through the Word (John 1:1–3). An intelligent creation gives meaning and purpose to the universe.

God	God is impersonal and is contained within all of existence (pantheism). Material reality is imbued with consciousness. God is all that really exists.	God is personal. He is both transcendent over his creation (Psalms 103:19) and immanent in relationship to creation (Psalms 72:19). The glory of God is revealed through his creation (Romans 1:19, 20), and yet to confuse God with his creation is scripturally condemned (Romans 1:25).
Man	Man, as a part of the one reality, is inherently divine. God is individualized in man. Man has evolved to a position of supremacy over the rest of existence.	The God of the Bible is the only true God (Isaiah 43:10; Jeremiah 10:10, 11). Man is highly exalted because of special creation in God's image (Genesis 1:26). The New Age looks within and worships the image, which is idolatry (Exodus 20:5; Romans 1:23).
Ethics	Man is good by nature. Through cosmic consciousness, categories of moral good and evil are transcended.	Morality is centered in man. The Bible views good and evil in antitheses. Revelation condemns the synthesizing of good and evil (Isaiah 5:20, 21). God is the absolute, transcendent moral standard as revealed in his Word. Man is in a condition of sin (Romans 3:23) and in need of a Savior (John 3:16; Hebrews 7:25).
Revelation	Propositional revelation is a barrier to spiritual enlightenment. Direct mystical states are the norm in the New Age.	Propositional revelation (Bible) is verbally inspired (II Timothy 3:16). Biblical revelation is historical. Therefore, Christianity can be tested relative to truth claims. Christianity is a rational faith which is intellectually defensible. Revelation leads to true spirituality.
History	History is cyclical. Man creates and directs the course of history independent of any transcendent reality.	The infinite God intercedes in space, time, and history. God orders history in fulfillment of his purposes. Man is significant in history and is a part of God's destined plan. History is meaningful.
Salvation	Man needs a transformation of consciousness (cosmic consciousness). Apart from cosmic consciousness, reincarnation is necessary. Man must save himself. Death is an illusion.	The heart of man is desperately wicked through sin (Jeremiah 17:9). Jesus Christ is God incarnate (John 1:1, 14). Man must be transformed (born again) through Jesus Christ (John 3:3). Man is saved by grace (Eph. 2:8). Death followed by judgment is a reality (Hebrews 9:27).

World Religions	All roads lead to God. There is no basis for comparative religions. All religions emanate from the same source.	Religious syncretism is irrational, for all religions do not teach the same things. This denies a common source for the world's religions.
Eschatology	Man will give birth to the New Age through his own consciousness (occult view of reality). Man is aided by spirit "guides" in his quest to consciously create a new heaven and a new earth.	The Second Coming of the Lord Jesus Christ will result in the new heaven and the new earth under his righteous reign (Revelation 21:1–8). Spirit "guides" are malignant spiritual entities (demons) that deliver spiritual delusion and a rejection of the one true God (II Thessalonians 2:8–12).

Notes to Chapter 1

1. Matthew Ralston, "She's Having the Time of Her Lives," *People Weekly*, January 26, 1987, p. 31.

2. Ibid., p. 30.

3. Elliot Miller, "The New Age Movement—What Is It?" *People Weekly*, January 26, 1987, p. 31.

4. Ibid., p. 20.

5. Norman Geisler, *Christian Apologetics* (Grand Rapids: Baker, 1976), p. 248.

6. David Spangler, *Revelation: The Birth of a New Age* (Middletown: Lorian, 1976), p. 195.

7. Maureen Orth, "The Sunshine Boy," *Newsweek*, Dec. 20, 1976.

8. Brooks Alexander, "The Rise of Cosmic Humanism: What Is Religion?" *SCP Journal*, Winter 1981–82, p. 3.

9. Ibid.

10. Francis A. Schaeffer and C. Everett Koop, *Whatever Happened to the Human Race?* (Old Tappan: Fleming H. Revell, 1979), p. 148.

11. Marilyn Ferguson, *The Aquarian Conspiracy* (Los Angeles: J. P. Tarcher, Inc., 1980), p. 371.

12. James Sire, *The Universe Next Door* (Downers Grove, InterVarsity Press, 1976), p. 172.

13. Spangler, *Revelation: The Birth of a New Age*, p. 211.

14. Ibid., p. 191.

15. Ralston, "She's Having the Time of Her Lives," p. 33.

16. John Lilly, *The Center of the Cyclone: An Autobiography of Inner Space* (New York: Julian Press, 1972), p. 210.

17. George B. Leonard, "Aikido and the Mind of the West," *Intellectual Digest*, June 1973, p. 20.

18. Ralston, "She's Having the Time of Her Lives," p. 33.

19. Ibid., p. 33.

20. Katherine Lowry, "Channelers," *Omni*, October 1987, p. 148.

21. Mark Vaz, "Psychic! The Many Faces of Kevin Ryerson" (interview), *Yoga Journal*, July/Aug. 1986, p. 28. Quoted in Elliot Miller, "Channeling Spiritistic Revelations for the New Age," *Christian Research Journal*, Fall 1987, p. 13.

22. Quoted by Tom Minnery, "Unplugging the New Age," *Focus on the Family*, August 1987, p. 3.

23. Reincarnation should not be confused with transmigration. Transmigration is the belief that the soul can return to inhabit any number of things in existence including animals, rocks, trees, etc. Reincarnation is considerably more acceptable to the Western mind.

24. Ralston, "She's Having the Time of Her Lives," p. 32

25. Benjamin Creme, *The Reappearance of the Christ and the Masters of Wisdom* (Hollywood: Tara Center, Undated pamphlet).

26. *Eerdmans' Handbook to the World's Religions* (Grand Rapids: Eerdmans, 1982), p. 31

27. Mircea Eliade, *The Sacred and the Profane*, trans. William R. Trask (New York: Harper & Row, 1952), pp. 122–23.

28. See Josh McDowell and John Gilchrist, *The Islam Debate* (San Bernardino: Here's Life Publishers, Inc. 1983), for insight into the many inconsistencies within Islam relative to truth claims.

29. Adapted from Harold O. J. Brown, *Heresies* (Garden City, N.Y.: Doubleday, 1984), p. 15.

30. See Josh McDowell, *Evidence That Demands A Verdict* (San Bernardino: Here's Life Publishers, Inc., 1979), chapter 9, "The Messianic Prophecies of the Old Testament Fulfilled in Jesus Christ," pp. 141–76. In this chapter, McDowell documents some 332 distinct prophecies literally fulfilled in Jesus of Nazareth.

31. John Warwick Montgomery, *The Shape of the Past* (Ann Arbor: Edwards Brothers, 1962), p. 140.

32. Spangler, *Revelation: The Birth of a New Age*, p. 121.

33. Mark and Elizabeth Clare Prophet, *Climbing the Highest Mountain* (Los Angeles: Summit Lighthouse, 1975), p. xxvi.

34. Creme, *The Reappearance of the Christ and the Masters of Wisdom*, p. 120.

35. Ibid., p. 25.

36. Shirley MacLaine, *Out on a Limb* (New York: Bantam Books, 1983), p. 91.

37. Levi Dowling, *The Aquarian Gospel of Jesus the Christ* (Marina del Rey: De Vorss & Co., 1964), p. 255.

38. Ibid., p. 261.

39. Dharma is a Buddhist doctrine. Dharma refers both to the moral and physical laws governing the universe and to the individual parts of the universe. The universe and everything in it are perceived as originating through the working together of the separate components in existence known as "dharmas." The human being only appears to be an individual; in reality, this is an illusion. The person is rather a part of flowing, continually changing dharmas, which following death rearranges itself to form a new individual.

40. Ferguson, *The Aquarian Conspiracy*, p. 100.

41. Ibid., p. 164.

42. Jessica Lipnack and Jeffrey Stamps, *Networking* (Garden City: Double-day, 1982), p. 7.

43. Teilhard de Chardin, *The Phenomenon of Man* (New York: Harper & Row, 1961), p. 3.

44. Ferguson, *The Aquarian Conspiracy*, p. 217.

45. Ibid., pp. 62–63.

46. Ibid., p. 25.

47. Ibid., p. 157.

48. Fritjof Capra, *The Turning Point* (Toronto: Bantam Books, 1982), p. 22.

49. Ferguson, *The Aquarian Conspiracy*, p. 28.

50. These lines are from the musical *Hair.*

2 | Escape from Reason

The insidious relativism of atheistic secular humanism has decayed values, social structures, and institutions in Western civilization. Secular humanism has left Western culture gasping for its last breath of meaning.

The pluralism that characterizes our culture has plunged the nation into a morass of religio-philosophical alternatives for the ailments of our society. In this "post–Christian era" in which we live, objective truth is rejected; truth is subjectivity. With no transcendent, absolute standard, people are blindly committing themselves to bizarre, shallow beliefs.

An occult tumult of unprecedented proportions has shaken Western civilization. The pendulum of Western thought has swung from the exaltation of reason to the widespread rejection of reason, from rationalism to mysticism, from materialism to the occult. "Yesterday's skeptics are some of today's firmest believers."[1]

This chapter will trace Western thought from the European Enlightenment, contemporary with the founding of America, to the present to explain this occult resurgence and to answer the question, Why are masses of people in twentieth-century America transcending conventional categories in pursuit of a spiritual journey into New Age mysticism?

The Age of Reason

The Enlightenment of the eighteenth century was characterized by the exaltation of human reason. Reason was exalted as the supreme

Sovereign over the affairs of men. Man sacrificed to reason, believing that within himself, he could find ultimate meaning and the reality of utopia. Man, and his finite reason, became the standard of truth. This meant that there was no need of a revelation from God. God was to be observed only in nature. Although reason was exalted and God was to be observed only in nature, the eighteenth-century thinker did not deny the existence of a personal God. The single banner of the Enlightenment was deism. Deism stresses the transcendence of God to the denial of his immanence. In deism, God is viewed as being beyond the world, a divine "First Cause" who has abandoned man to work out his own destiny.

The Enlightenment thinkers were optimistic about working out their own destiny, for in their view, man and society were perfectible. Man would finally realize his full potential and moral development in the "Age of Reason."

Since God did not intercede in human affairs, according to the Enlightenment thinkers, the universe was considered to be a closed system where miracles were impossible. It is noteworthy that this view did not originate because of scientific facts, but rather was rooted in the philosophical rationalism of the eighteenth century. John Toland, an English deist, represented this line of reasoning: "Whatever is evidently repugnant to clear and distinct ideas, or our common notions, is contrary to reason."[2]

If the universe is closed to God and his supernatural intervention, it is also closed to man's reordering of it. This results in a devaluation of man and renders free will as illusory. Man, to be able to reorder the world in which he lives, would necessarily have to transcend the natural order of cause and effect. The thinkers of the Enlightenment avoided such an assault to the dignity of man and continued to assume, as men will apart from reflection, that it was possible for them to maintain the hope of personal and social perfectibility.

As previously mentioned, the Enlightenment man believed that God was observable only in nature and, therefore, this was all that was needed to understand God. General revelation was then the basis for ethics; and since the world was not fallen, in the thinking of eighteenth-century man, then nature reveals whatever is right.

This view actually destroys ethics. If whatever is (in nature) is right, then evil is an illusion. Right and wrong, good and evil, are indistinguishable. This notion conflicts with man's own sense of justice and is therefore inconsistent with normal human experience.

Towards the end of the European Enlightenment in Germany, a brilliant thinker arose who has impacted thinking into the twentieth century. In his work, *Critique of Pure Reason*, Immanuel Kant was most concerned with the issue of man's ability to discover knowledge of reality in the estranged world of metaphysics. Metaphysics was considered alien because of the prevailing world view of deism.

Kant divided the natural world and the supernatural world into two distinct categories. He referred to these categories as the "phenomena" (the natural world as perceived by the human senses) and the "noumena" (the metaphysical or supernatural world that transcends human sensibilities). Kant reasoned that knowledge was only attainable through human experience that was grounded in reason. Human experience was limited to the empirical world of sensibility and therefore, the noumena (metaphysical world) was unintelligible and was without meaning. The primary contribution of noumena is its contrast to phenomena and the assignment of categories of knowledge to sense objects in the physical world.

In Jean-Jacques Rousseau, a French-speaking Swiss from Geneva, and Immanuel Kant we begin to see a swing from the optimism of the early Enlightenment thinkers to cynicism. To Rousseau, man was basically good in his primitive state, but the trappings and accretions of civilization had corrupted him. Civilization, to Rousseau, brought about inequality and evil. In his book *Discourse on the Arts and Sciences*, Rousseau accuses civilization of being the origin of evil:

> astronomy is born of superstition, eloquence of ambition, hatred, falsehood and flattery; geometry of avarice; physics of an idle curiosity; and even moral philosophy of human pride. Thus the arts and sciences owe their birth to our vices.[3]

The humanist problem of the earlier Enlightenment developed to the point that the universe, including man, was seen as a predetermined machine. Man was trapped in his own closed system.

An outraged Rousseau cried, "man was born free, but everywhere he is in chains!"[4]

The human dilemma decried by Kant and Rousseau led to an emphasis upon human experience and feeling. Another by-product was a movement away from the extreme significance placed upon reason at the beginning of the Enlightenment. However, the thinking of man was still rationalistic, and spiritual realities were relegated to the realm of the non-rational (noumena).

The European Enlightenment was contemporary with the political-cultural founding of America. Many of our founding fathers were directly influenced by the optimism of the Enlightenment in their quest for utopia. And in common with the Enlightenment, Thomas Paine, Thomas Jefferson, George Washington, and Benjamin Franklin, among others, were deists. There were, of course, orthodox Christian voices in the founding of America, such as Presbyterian clergyman John Witherspoon and General John Peter Muhlenberg.

Man, the Measure of Truth

The closed, determined universe of deism eventually led to the world view of naturalism in the West. As a result of deism, God is silent, there is no revelation, the Scriptures die. In naturalism, God is reduced to non-existence. In the absence of revelation, God cannot be known and he is slain in the thinking of men just as the Scriptures were in the previous century.

With no infinite God for man to look to for final reality, man becomes ultimate in the quest for meaning in life. This is what we mean when we speak of secular (non-theistic) humanism. This understanding of secular humanism is adapted from the ancient Greek philosopher Protagoras, who said, "man is the measure of all things." Humanistic man is alone in his universe.

The origin of the universe is explained in terms of evolution within the naturalistic world view. Matter exists eternally. For the naturalist, all matter in the universe has always existed in one form or another. Julien Offray de La Mettrie explains that, "In the whole universe there is but a single substance with various modifications."[5] The cosmos is ultimately of one essence and has no relationship to a transcendent God. Final reality in naturalism is merely matter, shaped by chance. The world has no ultimate explanation.

The universe, according to naturalism, is a uniform closed system of cause and effect. This is contrary to the perceptions of the early scientists (Copernicus, Galileo, Bacon, etc.) who believed in the concept of the uniformity of natural causes in an open system. In this concept, God and man are outside of the cause and effect machine of the cosmos. Through transcendence of the system, God and man are able to reorder the system. God is seen as providentially acting in history, and man is significant in this world view. In a closed universe, miracles are impossible. All events within a purely naturalistic world require a natural explanation. Paul Kurtz, editor of the *Humanist Manifesto I and II*, suggests:

> Any account of nature should pass the tests of scientific evidence; in our judgment, the dogmas and myths of traditional religions do not do so. . . . We find insufficient evidence for belief in the existence of a supernatural; it is either meaningless or irrelevant to the question of the survival and fulfillment of the human race. As nontheists, we begin with humans not God, nature not deity.[6]

Conclusively, for the secular humanist, "no deity will save us; we must save ourselves."[7]

Man is the accidental product of evolved nonintelligent mass and is reduced to machine, only one more part in the closed system of cause and effect. He is not a special creation as in the Judeo-Christian world view, but rather the accidental result of psychological and chemical conditioning. There is no overarching meaning and purpose to life in a determined universe. Indeed, free will is an illusion. Ethics are restricted to the subjective judgments of the individual. The relativistic thinking of secular humanism rejects any notion of an ultimate right and wrong, truth or error. The contemporary confusion of the concepts of ethics and morals has resulted in the rapid degeneration of our culture. A distinction must be made between these two concepts.[8]

Ethics (Greek: *ēthikos*) is a normative science. As a normative science, ethics is concerned with the standards (norms) employed to evaluate the value system of a culture. This means that ethics is concerned with the way things "ought" to be within a given culture.

Morality is a descriptive science and therefore is concerned with describing behavior within a given culture. Moral actions describe what people actually do and therefore "isness" rather than "oughtness" is intrinsic to the nature of morals. Hence, ethics is not concerned with what we do, as are morals, but rather ethics is concerned with what we ought to do.

The confusion of these concepts (ethics and morals) has resulted in like-minded people determining what is right and wrong within our society. Issues of right and wrong or even what is normal are therefore determined on the basis of what people enjoy doing rather than what they ought to be doing. For example, at my undergraduate university in the late sixties, the vast majority of students smoked marijuana. "Pot" smoking was then normal and "what is normal is good." Does the acceptance of a practice by a given culture make it right? This is the crux of our present social crisis.

When the normal (relating to morals) becomes the normative (relating to ethics), then the present "isness" (the way things are) of a culture determines what "ought" to be. This is in contradiction to the biblical ethic that determines the legitimacy of "isness" by what is ultimately right as founded upon the character of the transcendent God. A nation such as America, entrapped in this confusing dilemma, wallows in the filthy mire of its own moral depravity, claiming with relativistic blindness that evil is good and good is evil.

Herbert Spencer, who actually introduced the phrase "survival of the fittest," extended Charles Darwin's theory of the biological evolution of all life to include ethics. "Social Darwinism" became the basis for determining the worth of certain classes and races of people. The ethic of "strength over weakness" was the impetus for the hideous war crimes of Hitler and the Third Reich.[9] Hitler determined that the ideal was a super race of Germanic people and that it was morally expedient to strain the human race of Jewish blood and also of both mental and physical invalids. The relativity of moral action and the confusion of ethical/moral categories leaves the secular humanist with no objective ground upon which to judge such atrocities against human nature. In fact, many proponents of genetic engineering in contemporary America use similar arguments to support the position that the weak should not be kept alive by medical technology just to produce a "weaker" next generation.[10]

Professor Steven Weinberg, of Harvard University and the Smithsonian Astrophysical Observatory, eulogizes naturalism:

> It is very hard to realize that this all is just a tiny part of an overwhelmingly hostile universe . . . (which) has evolved from an unspeakably unfamiliar early condition, and faces a future extinction of endless cold or intolerable heat. The more the universe seems comprehensible, the more it also seems pointless.[11]

Atheistic philosopher Friedrich Nietzche proclaimed, "God is dead." Without ultimate meaning and purpose in life, so is man. This is nihilism, the grave of naturalism. Confronted with the hopeless despair of nihilism, man will reject reason and escape into the irrational in his search for meaning and purpose in life.

Existentialism: A Blind Leap!

"A literature of despair is a contradiction in terms. . . . In the darkest depths of our nihilism I have sought only for the means to transcend Nihilism," wrote an anxious Albert Camus.[12] Existentialism is modern man's answer to the despair of nihilism. Existentialism is represented in two strains: theistic and secular (atheistic). Soren Kierkegaard (1813–55), a Danish philosopher and a Christian, is the father of existential thought.

Existentialism (whether we are speaking of theistic or atheistic) is best defined through appeal to its principle premise, "existence is prior to essence." This is contrary to traditional thought (inclusive of biblical thought) which states, "essence is prior to existence." For the existentialist, human nature is determined by personal life experiences instead of human nature interpreting and determining life. In other words, my personal self-worth is contingent upon my performance, which grows out of my personal choices. I must create my own personal self-worth; human dignity is not intrinsic to human life. Therefore, through personal achievement the athlete (as perceived by American cultural values) possesses greater personal self-worth than the non-athlete. The Marine is more of a man than the non-Marine, or the professional woman attains to a greater degree of personal dignity than the housewife. The wealthy, of course, are of greater value than the poor.

Existentialists are primarily concerned with change, freedom, and self-cognizance as human values. To the existentialist, "truth is subjectivity." The external, objective world is considered to be philosophically absurd. Therefore, the only validation one needs of what is true is an inner sense of truthfulness. Truth does not conform to any transcendent objective standard.

Based on their premise "truth is subjectivity," proponents of atheistic existentialism (most prominent among them are Jean-Paul Sartre [1905–81], Martin Heidegger [1889–1971], and Karl Jaspers [1883–1969]) stressed that there are as many interpretations of truth as there are individuals in the world. Subjectivity is further understood in a "creative" sense. In other words, as illustrated above, man creates his own personal significance as an autonomous being.

Because "truth is subjectivity," all existentialists deny any distinction between subject and object. The objective world, as absurd or meaningless, is deemphasized. This diminishes the value of "intellectual knowledge" attained through the understanding and rather emphasizes the significance of gaining true knowledge via personal experience.

Existentialism did not fully impact Western thought until well into the twentieth century. This was because nihilism had not yet run its dreadful course and had not started to affect the lives and attitudes of the general populace.

World War I failed to make the world safe for democratic ideals. The rise of National Socialism in Germany, characterized by a denouncement of human dignity, provoked students and intellectuals worldwide to embrace such godless forms of thought as the meaninglessness of man and the absurdity of the objective world. Cultural despair, disillusionment, and human resignation provided fertile ground for atheistic existentialism. Contemporary Western thought is witnessing the full impact of this form of existentialism in that its denial of the transcendent God is ultimately nihilism in "sheep's clothing."[13]

Atheistic existentialism is principally concerned with man, who he is, and what his relationship to the world is. This is the starting point for atheistic existentialism's system of ethics. In a revolt against the absurd objective world, man must create value. It is not important that man's chosen values be measured against any absolutes, it only matters that man makes choices. The existentialist assumes that the choices made are ultimately the right choices, because according to this world view, man creates himself freely as presupposed by the premise "existence precedes essence." Because man creates his own value by his choices, it is assumed that he creates only that which is good. Meaning, for the existentialist, is then subjectively created in the face of a cruel, absurd world. "The meaning of a man's life consists in proving to himself every minute he is a man and not a piano key."[14] The dignity of man is founded upon his personal choices and through engaging himself in social activity: "I am creating a certain image of man of my own choosing. In choosing myself, I choose man."[15] According to Jean-Paul Sartre, the existentialist creates value and meaning not only for himself but for others as well.[16] Sartre observes that an individual's choices may not be desirable by others even though they are for the purpose of mutual well-being.[17]

James Sire is correct in his observation that some external standard must be recognized for the purpose of shaping proper moral behavior between "subjects."[18] Further, the subjectivism of atheistic existentialism fails to provide a transcendent standard necessary to distinguish reality from unreality. The objective world is continually imposing itself upon the subjective world of the existentialist forcing him to "forever affirm and affirm and affirm; when affirmation ceases, so does authentic existence."[19]

Soren Kierkegaard's writings did not become influential until after his death when they were translated into other languages. His writings encouraged the individual to consider new belief systems as a part of one's impassioned quest for the ultimate religious experience. True inner peace should characterize the attainment of this spiritual quest.

Instead of Jesus Christ, Kierkegaard begins with man in his quest to know God experientially, which requires a blind existential "leap of faith" on behalf of the seeker. Rather than returning to the religious thought of the Reformation (sixteenth century) Kierkegaard reacted against the dead orthodoxy of his day present within the liberal church in Denmark.

Since "truth is subjectivity," Kierkegaard holds objectivity to be uncertain, including propositional revelation, and insists that truth is gained by obedience, never observation. "A leap of faith" is the only means by which the true believer can embrace truth, according to Kierkegaard. Truth is the experience of human life and knowledge is the fruit of that experience.

The historical validation of the Christian faith (including the Bible) is deemphasized in theistic existentialism. Theistic existentialism is concerned with man's present existence and his own personal validation of his faith through individual choice. The death and resurrection of Jesus Christ are not for the atonement of man by the God-man but rather are for a new life of human service and sacrifice toward fellow man. Christian conversion was replaced by the arbitrary authenticating choices of man in the performance of benevolent works. The incarnation of Jesus Christ became mythological rather than historical fact.[20]

In his passionate search for ultimate meaning, the existentialist (theistic and atheistic alike) rejects reason. Meaning, faith, and values are placed in the realm of the non-rational. The only important thing is an undefinable, unverifiable experience that will bring the individual some sense of meaning.

As drugs became acceptable as a means to an unverifiable experience, the message of many rock music groups became influential upon the thinking of millions of western youth. Francis Schaeffer comments:

This emphasis on hallucinogenic drugs brought with it many rock groups, for example, Cream, Jefferson Airplane, Grateful Dead, Incredible String Band, Pink Floyd, and Jimi Hendrix. Most of their work was from 1965 to 1968. The Beatles' "Sergeant Pepper's Lonely Hearts Club Band" (1967) also fits here. This disc is a total unity, not just an isolated series of individual songs, and for a time it became the rallying cry for young people throughout the world. It expressed the essence of their lives, thinking, and feeling. As a whole, this music was the vehicle to carry the drug culture and the mentality which went with it across frontiers which were almost impassable by other means of communication.[21]

Psychedelic rock music became extremely popular in the sixties as a means to an ultimate experience without the use of drugs. The taking of drugs was more for the purpose of ideological development in a religious sense rather than as a means of escape as in the past.

Millions of young people were revolting against the empty values of their parents in the sixties in their search for meaning and values. It was right for young people to reject the empty values of their parents; however, the corrupt means they used only led to further disillusionment.

In the summer of 1969 a huge rock festival was held in the northeastern part of the United States. This rock concert was believed to be the ideological zenith of the drug counterculture of the sixties. It ended in tragedy. Francis Schaeffer reflects on Woodstock:

Many young people thought that Woodstock was the beginning of a new and wonderful age. The organizer claimed, "This is the beginning of a new era. It works!" But the drug world was already ugly, and it was approaching the end of its optimism, although the young people did not yet know it. Jimi Hendrix (1942–70) himself was soon to become a symbol of the end. Black, extremely talented, inhumanly exploited, he overdosed in September 1970 and drowned in his own vomit, soon after the claim that the culture of which he was a symbol was a new beginning. In the late sixties the ideological hopes based on drug taking died.[22]

Woodstock and other such festivals brought only further disenchantment as hope and meaning alluded the counterculture. The ritualistic drug taking of the counterculture was abandoned and drug taking was again for the purpose of escape.

Activism on college and university campuses, with its shouts of "anti-establishment," "anti-war," "anti-authority," etc. calmed to a listless silence. The silence was tormenting for in place of activism was apathy. The counterculture of the sixties sold out to its own set of empty values in parallel with those of its parents.

After the turmoil of the sixties, many thought that it was so much better when the universities quieted down in the early seventies. I could have wept. The young people had been right in their analysis, though wrong in their solutions. How much worse when many gave up hope and simply accepted the same values as their parents—personal peace and affluence. Now drugs remain, but only in parallel to the older generation's alcohol, and an excessive use of alcohol has become a problem among the young people as well. Promiscuous sex and bi-sexuality remain, but only in parallel to the older generation's adultery. In other words, as the young people revolted against their parents, they came around in a big circle—and often ended an inch lower—with only the same two impoverished values: their own kind of personal peace and their own kind of affluence.[23]

Hedonism is the god of modern man. Hedonism is the attempt to find temporary pleasure in anything that will satisfy. Narcissism (the view that everything exists for an individual's pleasure) is the impetus for modern hedonistic man as he desperately seeks an escape from the despair of a godless humanistic culture void of any absolutes necessary to give meaning to life. The irrational then becomes an alternative for modern hedonistic man and his insatiable appetite for pleasure.

Whereas theistic existentialism leads to neo-orthodoxy in theology, atheistic existentialism and the drug counterculture that it inspired became an open door into the irrational, illusory realm of non-reason. The West was destined to wed with the East.

The Marriage of East and West

The turning of masses in the West to the imported mysticism of the East was preceded by modern man's escape from reason and by his rejection of the Judeo-Christian world view. In the face of widespread intellectual suicide, the East made an unprecedented debut in the West.

> With its antirationalism, its syncretism, its quietism, its lack of technology, its uncomplicated lifestyle and its radically different religious framework, the East is extremely attractive.[24]

The Bhagavad Gita, the Rig Veda, the Ramayana, the Pali Canon, and the Tibetan Book of the Dead are now common reading for millions of Westerners.

Many individuals were influential in the matrimony of the East and the West. Among the leading figures was Alan Watts, who taught for many years at San Francisco's School of Asian Studies. Watts authored seven books on Zen Buddhism before he was thirty-five years old. Zen became very attractive to the antinomian turned apathetic. Zen's view of sin as the result of man's desire to see change through revolt is particularly acceptable to a resigned rebel:

> The real human tragedy began when nature was to be dominated by man, for when the idea of power, which is domination, comes in, all kinds of struggles arise.[25]

> The escapism of the East is the path chosen by those seeking ultimate reality apart from rational thought. The post–Christian West is very susceptible to Eastern thought because of many parallels in their mutual concepts of ultimate reality. Both agree together that ultimate reality is summed up by two basic alternatives: "sheer silence" or a "mere symbolism" of mysticism.[26]

Here is where Immanuel Kant's influence upon Western thought becomes very apparent. As previously mentioned, Kant insisted that knowledge was attainable only in the "phenomenal" world (physical world of sensibility) and the "noumenal" world was unknowable (metaphysical realm). Therefore, the supernatural is irrational. Ludwig Wittgenstein extended Kant's thinking at this point and concluded that to speak of God was meaningless because God is a part of the unknowable metaphysical realm (noumena). According to Wittgenstein, "Whereof one cannot speak, thereof one must be silent."[27] This is the "sheer silence" of Western philosophy (this type of philosophy is referred to as linguistic analysis).

The other alternative is the "mere symbolism" of liberal theology. The Bible is not God's self-revelation to man, according to liberalism, but it is rather man's interpretation of God. The Bible is merely symbolic truth. Faith is divorced from facts or reason. History is a myth. Therefore, the "higher critics" of liberalism responded, with their historical scalpels in hand, and proceded to amputate ("demythologize") the meaningless statements about the supernatural from the Bible.

Liberalism chose to replace historical Christianity with its own myth. In liberal "Christian" thought, the church created a supernatural Jesus through its doctoring of the New Testament documents in the second and third centuries. There was no room for a resurrected, ascended, supernatural Jesus creating the church on the day of Pentecost (Acts 2). The myth of liberalism takes its place alongside any other world religion with no greater claim to truth.

Karl Barth, a Swiss theologian, introduced the existential method into theology (this is known as neo-orthodoxy). The old liberalism had failed. Barth had held to the "higher critical" views of liberalism and therefore had concluded that the Bible was errant until towards the end of his life. He then taught that a religious "word" could existentially (subjectively) break through from the Bible and actually become the Word of God.

In neo-orthodoxy, the Bible is fallible in the area of reason (phenomena) but one can have a religious experience in the area of the irrational (noumena). Neo-orthodoxy does not place faith in an objective personal God but rather it encourages an individual to have faith in one's faith. The Word of God is really without content. Experience alone brings content to the Bible in neo-orthodoxy.

The "mere symbolism" of liberalism represents the failure of Christianity to many people in the West and opens the door to the mystical religions of the East. God is unknowable in the Eastern occult world view of religions such as Hinduism and Buddhism. Any descriptive term applied to God ends in reducing him to our own understanding; therefore, God cannot be known through verbal propositional revelation (i.e., the Bible). God is to be known only through the intuitive awareness of meditation, through direct mystical states. In the silence of the East, verification of spiritual realities is via participation.

Vedic Hinduism views Brahman, the infinite impersonal deity, as final reality. The concept "God" is understood in terms of pantheism. Pantheism, as discussed in chapter one, confuses God with creation. All that is, is God, and anything that appears to exist apart from God is maya, or illusion.

The blending of East and West has spawned the human potential movement. The human potential movement encourages the exploration of new inner frontiers for the purpose of realizing our full potential.

The Three-Pound Universe

Boldly ascending conventional categories, the human potential movement ventures into the inner space of the human ego in order to discover the boundaries of this vast universe, if in fact any boundaries do exist.

Abraham Maslow introduced the theme of unrealized human potential into humanistic psychology in the 1950s. Maslow coined the term "self-actualization" as applied to unrealized human potential. Carl Rogers joined Maslow in expressing that "ideally, the organism is always endeavoring to actualize itself."[28] In the early 1900s, Carl Jung preceded both Maslow and Rogers in campaigning for unrealized human potential. Jung used the term "individuation process" to describe man's quest for fulfillment.

In the 1970s, the search for unrealized human potential was launched into the infinite. Psychospiritual type cults like est (Erhard Seminars Training now known as the Forum) Lifespring, Silva Mind Control, Scientology, and others expressed the common belief that man was suffering from spiritual amnesia. Man's true identity must be realized in cosmic terms. God is man's autobiography. Man must learn to pay obeisance at the proper altar, his mirror. The conscious evolution of modern man, sparked by the human potential movement, has awakened humanity to "a new cultural myth."[29]

Conclusion

The rejection of reason in the twentieth century as a basis for understanding spiritual realities contributed to opening the door to the irrational spirituality of the occult in the West.

Additionally, the rejection of the supernatural by theological liberalism has caused masses to seek elsewhere for spiritual fulfillment. The unfounded assaults upon biblical revelation by liberalism resulted in the loss of a critical standard by which to judge spiritual realities. This results in subjective experience as being the basis upon which to test spiritual phenomena. With no reliable, objective standard by which to judge spiritual phenomena, the occult is allowed to flourish unchecked. For many in the West, liberalism represents Christianity as being lifeless, powerless, and meaningless.

The social chaos of the counterculture, associated with widespread drug use, resulted in the departure of many from former traditional values. A general uncertainty as to personal identity and purpose in life has gripped our culture. Eastern occult-mysticism offers spiritually hungry man in the West ultimate answers as to his identity and purpose for being. Under the aegis of renewed hope, the occult encourages man to look within and discover his "true" nature. As modern man looks within in his search for purpose and spiritual understanding, he ends in bowing his knee in worship to the image of God instead of the image's Creator, the Sovereign God.

The idolatry of modern man is seemingly endorsed by large segments of humanistic psychology. The human potential movement, represented by such notables as Abraham Maslow, Carl Rogers, Carl Jung, and B. F. Skinner has sanctioned psychic and parapsychological research. Occult influence results in former concepts of human potential being perceived in infinite terms.

Contemporary socio-political disenchantment and future fear, particularly the annihilation of the planet through nuclear holocaust, ecological collapse, or other catastrophic means have served as the impetus for modern New Age man to be the avant-garde into new spiritual frontiers that will be the gateway into the Aquarian Age of global peace and ultimate human fulfillment. As occult influences are secularized (this results in their being demystified) within our culture via the myth of the New Age, "Their underlying themes run through contemporary science, economics, politics, art, psychology, and religion."[30]

Notes to Chapter 2

1. Os Guinness, *The Dust of Death* (Downers Grove: InterVarsity Press, 1973), p. 278.

2. Quoted in Geisler, *Christian Apologetics*, 1976, p. 157.

3. Quoted in Frederick Copleston, *A History of Philosophy*, vol. 6 (Garden City: Image, 1960), p. 80.

4. Quoted in Francis Schaeffer, *How Should We Then Live?* (Old Tappan: Fleming H. Revell, 1976), p. 155.

5. Julien Offray de La Mettrie, *Man a Machine (1747)*, in *Les Philosophes*, ed. Norman L. Torrey (New York: Capricorn Books, 1960), p. 177.

6. Paul Kurtz, ed. *Humanist Manifesto I and II* (Buffalo: Prometheus Books, 1973), pp. 15, 16.

7. Ibid., p. 16.

8. R. C. Sproul, Ligonier Ministries, has been particularly influential upon my thinking in this critical area. In his "Building a Christian Conscience" (a tape cassette album, copyright 1984 by Ligonier Ministries), Sproul brilliantly analyzes our contemporary cultural dilemma resulting from the confusion of morals and ethics.

9. Schaeffer, *How Should We Then Live?* p. 151.

10. Ibid., p. 151.

11. Quoted in Schaeffer and Koop, *Whatever Happened to the Human Race?* p. 135.

12. Quoted in Sire, *The Universe Next Door*, p. 99.

13. Josh McDowell and Don Stewart, *Handbook of Today's Religions* (San Bernardino: Here's Life Publishers, 1983), p. 481.

14. Fyodor Dostoevsky, *Notes From Underground* (New York: New American Library, 1961), p. 99.

15. Ibid.

16. Jean-Paul Sartre, "Existentialism," reprinted in *A Casebook on Existentialism*, ed. William V. Spanos (New York: Thomas Y. Crowell, 1966), p. 280.

17. Ibid.

18. Sire, *The Universe Next Door*, p. 108.

19. Ibid., pp. 112–13.

20. Ibid., p. 123.

21. Schaeffer and Koop, *Whatever Happened to the Human Race?* p. 170.

22. Schaeffer, *How Should We Then Live?* pp. 208–9.

23. Ibid., p. 210.

24. Sire, *The Universe Next Door*, pp. 130–31.

25. Walter Martin, *The Kingdom of the Cults* (Minneapolis: Bethany Fellowship, 1977), p. 238.

26. Guinness, *The Dust of Death*, pp. 203, 204.

27. Ibid., p. 202.

28. Frances Adeney, "The Flowering of the Human Potential Movement," *SCP Journal*, Winter 1981–82, p. 8.

29. Barry McWaters, *Conscious Evolution* (Los Angeles: New Age Press, 1981), p. xii, from the foreword by David Spangler.

30. Brooks Alexander, "Occult Philosophy and Mystical Experience," *SCP Journal*, Winter 1984, p. 14.

3 | A New Cultural Myth

Myths originate out of people's need to believe that they can conquer not only external enemies, but the often greater enemy of their own fear. A central motif of virtually all myths is the engendering of belief in personal and societal survival in the face of a fearsome world.

Myths are stories that allegorically reflect the spiritual foundations of a society. They are symbolic of human experience, reflecting a culture's values, prevailing beliefs, and world view. Myths therefore, have culturally formative power, and according to the late Joseph Campbell, one of the foremost authorities on mythology, they teach us, "how to live a human lifetime under any circumstances."[1] Myths seek to explain origins, natural phenomena, and death. They may also describe the nature, functions, and desires of the gods. The gods of myth are either represented in terms of individual deities or as forces of nature.

Campbell insists that we need myths. Myths are "bits of information from ancient times which have to do with the themes that have supported human life, built civilizations, and informed religions over the millennia." Myths provide understanding of "deep inner problems, inner mysteries, inner thresholds of passage."[2]

The New Myth

All myths share common themes that repeatedly inform cultures and form the spiritual ground for human experience. Citing the predictable nature of myths, Campbell insists that

Myths and dreams come from the same place. They come from reali-
zations of some kind that have then to find expression in symbolic form.
And the only myth that is going to be worth thinking about in the immediate future is one that is talking about the planet, not the city, not
these people, but the planet, and everybody on it. That's my main thought
for what the future myth is going to be.[3]

The ground of the New Myth must be a vision of a unified planetary
society.

Professors Irving Hexham and Karla Poewe-Hexham of the University of Calgary cite three mythic motifs characteristic of the New Age
myth: decline beliefs, New Age beliefs, and other civilization beliefs.[4]
Fears about nuclear holocaust and other cataclysmic events breed decline beliefs. A general attitude of pessimism provides a matrix for themes
of global destruction within decline beliefs. Religions, books, and movies
setting forth doomsday themes were widely received in the '60s and
'70s, a period when decline beliefs were very much in vogue.

Contrary to decline beliefs, New Age beliefs are extraordinarily
optimistic. The New Age myth announces the dawning of the Aquarian
Age (an age of great spiritual awareness when man will realize his unlimited potential, according to astrologers) following the pessimistic age
of Pisces (astrologers associate this period with Christianity). Optimism
in the face of dreadful gloom is a common mythic theme according
to Campbell: "One thing that comes out in myths, for example, is that
at the bottom of the abyss comes the voice of salvation. The black moment is the moment when the real message of transformation is going
to come. At the darkest moment comes the light."[5] The New Age is
a myth in the classic sense of mythology.

Other civilization beliefs "are concerned either with lost civilizations or extraterrestrial ones. They usually involve the suggestion, popu-
larized by Erich Von Daniken, that people in the remote past had contact
with extraterrestrial beings."[6] These beliefs generally are pre-historic accounts of the existence of super-races in utopian-like environments. The
gradual decline of these super-races results in the loss of the mystical
powers of mankind. The demi-gods of the lost continent of Atlantis
(made popular in the United States, among others, by Helena P. Blavatsky and Alice Bailey of the Theosophical Society) is a popular myth
of this type which includes the legends about Stonehenge, a mysterious
monument in southern England believed to have been constructed by
a Neolithic people some 4,100 years ago; the Egyptian pyramids; the
South American ruins of Machu Pichu in Peru. Hexham and Poewe-
Hexham further comment that "The purpose of these stories is to pro-

vide a powerful apologetic that links the meditative practices of New Age believers with apparent evidence that what they believe is true."[7]

The New Age apologetic is, however, based upon the logical fallacy of circular reasoning. The ancient ruins are said to provide evidence for the optimistic beliefs of the New Age which are linked to the doomsday themes of decline beliefs. The ruins represent realistic corresponding physical evidence for the mystical experiences and contacts with extraterrestrials claimed by many New Agers, such as Shirley MacLaine in her Peruvian adventures. Hexham and Poewe-Hexham further observe that "Similarly, the basis of hope in the face of prevailing pessimism would seem absurd without the 'reality' of mystic encounters. So a circle is forged, which becomes self-authenticating by providing a comprehensive mythological interpretation of life."[8]

The New Myth and Science

Many contemporary, influential scientists are thumbing a ride down the shamanistic highway of Carlos Castaneda.[9] The "mystic crystal revelations" of the new science will be revolutionary, according to theoretical physicist and systems theorist Fritjof Capra, "because the whole structure of our society does not correspond with the world-view of emerging scientific thought."[10]

These scientific revolutionaries are integrating modern physics with Eastern mysticism in a effort to hasten cultural transformation and the emergence of a new view of reality that will replace the mechanistic world view of mainstream scientific thought. "In contrast to the mechanistic Western view, the Eastern view of the world is 'organic,' " according to Capra.[11] The Eastern mystical world view perceives an interrelation of all the different aspects of the same ultimate reality.

The Cartesian division and the mechanistic world view (the Newtonian model) are considered reductionistic by the revolutionaries of the new science because they provide a model of a fragmented universe instead of a holistic model (monism). Capra cites this fragmented view of reality as the root cause of the current planetary crisis:

> This inner fragmentation mirrors our view of the world "outside," which is seen as a multitude of separate objects and events. The natural environment is treated as if it consisted of separate parts to be exploited by different interest groups. The fragmented view is further extended to so-

ciety, which is split into different nations, races, religious and political groups. The belief that all these fragments—in ourselves, in our government, and in our society—are really separate can be seen as the essential reason for the present series of social, ecological, and cultural crises. It has alienated us from nature and from our fellow human beings. It has brought a grossly unjust distribution of natural resources, creating economic and political disorder; an ever-rising wave of violence, both spontaneous and institutionalized, and an ugly, polluted environment in which life has often become physically and mentally unhealthy.[12]

Therefore, according to the agenda of the new science, our view of reality must keep pace with advancements in scientific knowledge. According to Capra, quantum theory and relativity theory,[13] the basis of modern physics, "force us to see the world very much in the way a Hindu, Buddhist, or Taoist sees it."[14] In seeking unity between spirit and matter, the new science has turned inward to the exploration of the "ultimate frontier" of the human consciousness. The human consciousness is believed to be the bridge between these formerly alien realities. The new science "attempts to suggest that modern physics goes far beyond technology, the way—or Tao—of physics can be a path with a heart, a way to spiritual knowledge and self-realization."[15]

The new science thus views the universe as one inseparable reality—a living organism—of which the observer is merely an extension. Capra comments on this subjective departure from the former empirical methods of scientific observation:

> As Eastern thought has begun to interest a significant number of people, and meditation is no longer viewed with ridicule of suspicion, mysticism is being taken seriously even within the scientific community. An increasing number of scientists are aware that mystical thought provides a consistent and relevant philosophical background to the theories of contemporary science, a conception of the world in which the scientific discoveries of men and women can be in perfect harmony with their spiritual aims and religious beliefs.[16]

A religious conversion must precede one's perception of the universe as one indivisible organic whole. Eastern mysticism then provides the scaffolding for the construction of the subjective science of the New Age.

The New Myth and Medicine

The subjective science of the New Age is the matrix for the holistic health movement. Holistic medicine "is a novel American phenomenon that seems an odd mix of ancient religious rituals, invocations of nature spirits, and pantheistic philosophy."[17]

The holistic model conceives of mind, body, and spirit as being one inseparable whole. Health is not just a matter of the body overcoming disease, as with more conventional models, but rather holistic medicine prescribes a balance of "our emotional states of mind, our lifestyles, and the environments in which we live and work. When our body-minds are out of balance, we are literally 'dis-eased,' opening ourselves to pain and other symptoms that are manifestations of a more basic disorder."[18]

Patients are encouraged to look beyond physical symptoms to the broader context of illness such as stress, social pressures, family conflicts, dietary habits, seasonal changes, and emotional highs and lows. Pain and disease are then understood in terms of the disharmony of these elements of human experience. The new health paradigm is people-oriented instead of the technological orientation of conventional medicine.

A holistic approach to medicine includes a variety of diagnostic tools and treatments. Some of these are conventional, many are not. The various psychotechnologies employed in holistic medicine include biofeedback, acupuncture, chiropractic techniques, creative visualization, meditation, yoga, hypnosis, various schools of massage, rolfing, and other body therapies.

The psychotechnologies of holistic medicine are designed to invoke mystical states of mind. Kenneth Pelletier, Assistant Clinical Professor of Psychiatry at the University of California School of Medicine in San Francisco, openly states that the manipulation of the patient's world view by the practitioner through the use of the various psychotechnologies is a part of the healing process.

> A person entering into meditation has already in some sense committed himself to an accompanying philosophical system. This factor of the individual's attitude as he approaches meditation practice cannot be underestimated in understanding the positive effects of such practice.[19]

In keeping with the New Age world view, the psychotechnologies of holistic medicine aid in inducing a psychological construct that allows the "divine within each person" to be the source of healing.

The influence of the holistic health movement is rapidly growing in America. Marilyn Ferguson reports on its advance:

> The new way of thinking about health and disease, with its message of hope and its change of individual responsibility, is widely communicated

by the Aquarian Conspiracy, as in a 1978 Washington conference, "Holistic Health: A Public Policy," co-sponsored by several government agencies and private organizations. Agencies from the Department of Health, Education and Welfare were represented. So was the White House staff. Insurance companies, pre-paid health plan organizations, and foundations sent representatives—in many cases, their top executive officers. Politicians, physicians, psychologists, traditional healers, spiritual teachers, researchers, futurists, sociologists, and health policy makers shared the platform. The assistant surgeon-general opened the conference; principal speakers included Jerome Frank on the placebo effect, California legislator John Vasconcellos, meditation teacher Jack Schwarz, Buckminster Fuller on human ecology.[20]

The complete menu of psychotechnologies was discussed along with public health policy and the implementation of holistic health centers. The "changing image of man" was also a focus of the conference.

In 1975, Malcolm Todd, then president of the American Medical Association, assumed a defensive posture towards holistic medicine at a conference sponsored by the Menninger Clinic in Tucson, Arizona. According to Ferguson, less than a year later at a similar conference in San Diego, "Todd endorsed the concept of a 'humanistic medicine' that deals with the 'bodymind.' "[21] Nine months after the San Diego conference, Todd urged a well-attended conference of medical professionals in Houston to use holistic techniques in medicine.[22]

The American Holistic Medical Association estimates that 2% or ten-thousand U.S. doctors practice some form of holistic medicine.[23] A significant number of insurance companies now provide coverage for claims originating from holistic therapies. In 1987, the National Institutes of Health sponsored $70 million dollars worth of research in "behavioral medicine."[24]

Numerous retreats, conventions, expositions, and organizations, including The Center for Integral Medicine, The Institute of Humanistic Medicine, The Association for Holistic Health, and scores of holistic health centers and clinics, are all promoting the message of the holistic health movement in our society: "in finding health, we find ourselves."[25]

The New Myth and Politics

An individual view of holism must precede a global view of holism according to the political ideology of the New Age. "Healing ourselves, healing our planet: Both are indispensable for creating a more cooperative and sustainable society."[26]

The threat of nuclear holocaust "is the most dramatic symptom of a multifaceted, global crisis that touches every aspect of our lives: our health and livelihood, the quality of our environment and our social relationships, our economy, technology, our politics—our very survival on this planet."[27] New Age political activists are calling for the transformation of the former sociopolitical paradigm (the mechanistic world view) to their holistic system.

As with the new science, the current global crisis is attributed to a fragmented world view (mechanistic). A "radical revision" of human thought, capable of understanding and bringing resolutions to the complex global problems of our day, is necessary for the survival of our planet.

A global awareness that perceives of humanity "inclusively" instead of "exclusively" (meaning in terms of focusing only upon our own nation, community, race, or religion) is the priority of the New Age political agenda. Donald Keys, founder of Planetary Citizens, is an aggressive New Age political strategist. Keys asserts the need for a planetary perspective:

> There has to be some critical mass of public awareness of planetary consciousness before politicians will move, before foreign offices will get into gear, before teaching changes in the schools.[28]

"Planetization" is the vision of a unified global community set in the frame of New Age ideology and values. Elliot Miller observes that "The cause of planetization continually attracts new adherents in international circles. It has a broad base of support with the UN secretariat, and among disadvantaged and small countries in both hemispheres, public and private international organizations, and special interest groups. It is actively promoted by an international network of influential academics, industrialists, scientists, etc., such as those in the Club of Rome and the Institute for World Order."[29]

Fritjof Capra further attributes our societal and planetary ills to the fact that our culture is dominated by a patriarchal tradition.[30] A patriarchal orientation results in continual power struggles. Characteristic of patriarchal societies, according to Capra, is "a pathological obsession with 'winning' in a situation where the whole concept of winning has lost its meaning, because there can be no winners in a nuclear war."[31] Patriarchal societies engender an insatiable drive for power and dominance which are equated with masculinity, "and warfare is held to be the ultimate initiation into true manhood," according to Capra.[32]

Therefore, because of its supreme commitment to planetary survival, New Age politics has abandoned the patriarchal tradition in favor of a matriarchal tradition that engenders community instead of aggression, intuition instead of rationality, cooperation instead of domination. The "Earth Mother" is referred to as "Gaia" by many New Agers. The primordial earth goddess, Gaia, is the Great Mother of all the goddesses in Greek mythology.[33] The paganistic concept of an "Earth Mother" is compatible with the pantheistic view of the material universe held by the New Age myth. This view of the earth as a conscious organism explains the extreme dedication to ecological concerns by the New Age. Further, since mankind and the earth are essentially a part of one inseparable whole, according to pantheism, environmental conservation is equated with racial preservation.

Instead of following its custom of naming a "Man of the Year," the January 2, 1989, issue of *Time* magazine designated Earth as the "Planet of the Year." *Time* impresses the current ecological crisis of our planet upon its readers in stating that the Earth's "future is clouded by man's reckless ways: overpopulation, pollution, waste of resources and wanton destruction of natural habitats."[34]

The Green Movement is a growing, worldwide political entity informed by the New Myth. The Green Movement has grown out of a variety of sociopolitical movements (including, peace, women's rights and civil rights movements, and ecological issues). "In Europe there are even Green political parties – coalitions of holistic ideological, . . . ecological, peace, and Marxist factions," according to Miller.[35]

Self-government growing out of the New Age value of personal autonomy (or the ultimate deification of man) is the political ideal of a majority committed to the Aquarian myth. Networks, composed of either individuals or organizations, serve to bring people together who have shared political interests. Through networking, the commitment to a decentralized form of government, is best served. For many New Age activists "the use of networks has largely replaced political parties as a means of impacting public policy and the character of cultural life."[36]

The political aspirations of the New Myth were set forth by several "spiritual leaders" at the United Nations in October of 1975:

> The crises of our time are challenging the world religions to release a
> new spiritual force transcending religious, cultural, and national boun-

daries into a new consciousness of the oneness of the human community and so putting into effect a spiritual dynamic toward the solutions of the world's problems. . . . We affirm a new spirituality divested of insularity and directed toward planetary consciousness.[37]

There is a minority of New Agers committed to a centralized form of government. This minority looks for a messianic-type figure to be the world leader. This minority of New Agers is influenced, in large part, by the writings of Alice Bailey and Madam Helena Blavatsky of the Theosophical Society. Issues raised from the commitment to a centralized form of government by some New Agers are discussed at length in chapter seven.

The New Myth and Education

Education provides center stage for the reshaping of Western culture by the New Myth. "You can only have a new society, the visionaries have said, if you change the education of the younger generation."[38] The New Age model of educational philosophy is sometimes called "transpersonal education." The self-transcending themes of transpersonal education are illustrated in *How the Ewoks Saved the Trees. An Old Ewok Legend*, by James Howe.[39] This book, originating from George Lucas's *Star Wars* themes, is part of the reading curriculum for first graders in a Washington state public school.

The Ewoks are cute little cub-like creatures who live on a tiny obscure moon called Endor. Endor was covered with a very great forest. The Ewoks were nature worshippers. Each night, before going to sleep in their hammocks, these pagan creatures "chanted thanks to the trees that surrounded them."[40] The trees, which provide protection for the Ewoks in return, are said to be "living spirits" (this is the religious concept of animism) which possess the ability to speak (though they have not spoken for many generations).

Wicket and Princess Kneesaa are two Ewok children who have a perilous adventure. While picking berries in the woods, the two children suddenly hear strange, painful moans. The moans are preceded by another strange sound that echoes through the woods. The children decide to investigate the strange sounds. As they do, they soon discover two alien giants, who are chopping the trees down. The Ewoks consider this to be sacrilegious.

The two Ewoks wait for the giants to finish their day's work and lie down to sleep. The young Ewoks then approach the crying trees and begin to talk with them. The trees explain that the giants are known as Phlogs and they are from the land of Simoon on the other side of the moon of Endor.

The land of Simoon had suffered total ecological collapse at the hands of the Phlogs. There were no longer any trees in the land of Simoon so the Phlogs came to Endor to harvest the trees there.

The two children run home to alert the Ewok elders of the invasion of their land by the Phlogs. However, even though their planet is on the edge of ecological and ultimately, racial annihilation, the elders refuse to listen to the testimony of the children. The Ewok children must turn to a wizard, Logray. Although Logray is an Ewok, because of his peculiarities, he is representative of the fringe element of society. Logray believes the children's story.

Logray then uses a myth to explain the problem presently facing the Ewok race. Logray explains to the children that the Ewoks once lived in Simoon. The ecological destruction of Simoon forced the Ewoks to search out a new land for the sake of the survival of their race. Finally, the Ewoks discovered Endor and they have peaceably lived there ever since. Once again, however, the Phlogs are threatening the very survival of the Ewoks.

Fortunately, Logray has a plan that will save the Ewoks from apocalyptic doom. Logray practices alternative medicine as a means to treat the illnesses of the Ewok people. Logray reaches into his bag of esoteric cures and pulls out a magical powder that will make the giants forget why they ever came to Endor and this will result in the Phlogs leaving.

As the children set out to deliver the Ewoks and Endor from ultimate destruction, they run into a scouting party of the elder Ewoks led by Chief Chirpa, Princess Kneesaa's father. The elder Ewoks have finally decided to act upon the urgent pleas of the children. However, the elder Ewoks insist upon relying on their technology (i.e., bows and arrows, spears, and ropes) as a means to deal with the threat of the Phlogs. The methods of the elder Ewoks are futile. Rather, the heroic efforts of the children getting the Phlogs to ingest the magic powder results in the confusion of the giants and their leaving Endor. Old modes of dealing with problems (obsolete paradigms) are insufficient. New modes (a paradigm shift) must be used in order to save the planet. The new paradigm derives from the shunned fringe element of Ewok culture.

The story of the Ewoks closes with the "Medicine Man" (Logray) being received (with all of his peculiar methods and ways) into the mainstream of Ewok culture. The trees have not sung or spoken to the older Ewoks for generations. But suddenly, the songs of the trees fill the land of Endor.

Each year now, the Ewoks gather for the purpose of engaging in a ritualistic pagan chant:

> "Trees and Ewoks,
> Ewoks and Trees,
> Always will we help each other.
> Always will we live as one."[41]

The intuitive realization of our oneness (interconnectedness) with the universe results in transformation and the survival of the planet. The holistic world view of the Ewoks informs them of their autonomous ability to control their own reality.

"Transpersonal education" is a psychological term that emphasizes "the transcendent capacities of human beings."[42] The concept of self as an autonomous entity is at the root of transpersonal education. According to Ferguson, "In transpersonal education, the learner is encouraged to be awake and autonomous, to question, to explore all the corners and crevices of conscious experience, to seek meaning, to test outer limits, to check out frontiers and depths of the self."[43]

Frances Adeney provides an illuminating illustration of what is meant by public school students checking "out frontiers and depths of the self":

> Twenty-five first graders lie in motionless silence on the classroom floor. The teacher intones soothing phrases to aid relaxation. Within moments, the meditative journey begins. The children imagine the sun, shining its brightest, radiating intense light toward them. They gaze directly into it and despite its strength the sun's brightness doesn't hurt them. Then, in their mind's eye, the children are told to bring the sun down, down from the sky and into their own body. Its light pulses from head, down into chest regions, further and further until their body is ablaze with light. Now picture yourself doing something perfectly, says the teacher. Keep watching yourself being perfect. Fill yourself with the knowledge of being perfect. This is your light, your intelligence, your sun. Your whole body becomes a beam of light. The teacher tells them to see themselves full of light. Now contain all of the light in the universe. With that light, the teacher says, they now feel at peace—they are perfect. As they return from this fantasy journey, the children are reminded that

they are intelligent, magnificent, and that they contain all of the wisdom of the universe within themselves.[44]

This exercise in "guided imagery" took place in a Los Angeles public school. It is a part of the confluent educational curriculum developed by Dr. Beverly Galyean.

Confluent education is representative of a myriad of other curriculums informed by the New Age myth and designed to acquaint the student with the divine nature of their "higher self." The basic axioms of confluent education incorporate the mythic themes of the New Age as follows:

1. In essence we are not individuals but part of the universal consciousness, God or spirit, which has manifested itself in the material world. At its base, this universal consciousness is love. Realizing this essential unity, and experiencing oneself as part of it, is a major goal for a child's education.

2. Because each person is part of the universal consciousness which is love, each child contains all the wisdom and love of the universe. This wisdom and love is the "higher self." "My mind already knows how to spell these words," children are told to say to themselves. In being taught a sense of self-worth and self-confidence, children are directly told that they are perfect, all-loving, and all-wise. "I am a perfect person and student" is an expression which children are instructed to repeat to themselves frequently. The child can tap into this universal mind and receive advice, information, and help from it. This is usually done through meditation and contact with "spirit guides."

3. Each person creates his or her own reality by choosing what to perceive and how to perceive it. As we teach children to focus on positive thoughts and feelings of love, their reality will become that. This is an assumption that the physical world is illusion, that what we perceive is in our minds. That is, the truth of anything is not in its external existence, but in our subjective experience of it. Therefore, all of the students' activities are positive, and they are taught to "get in touch with their magnificence."[45]

This holistic approach to education introduces the student to "whole-brain knowing." Whole-brain knowing incorporates both the right and left hemispheres of the brain. The left side of the brain is analytical and is the hemisphere where logic and reason are engaged. The right side of the brain is the intuitive hemisphere. Transpersonal education seeks to harmonize both hemispheres of the brain. The New Age "Metaphor builds a bridge between the hemispheres, symbolically carrying knowledge from the mute right brain so that it may be recognized by the left as being like something already known."[46] This synthesis results in the right hemisphere providing a context for learning where the left hemisphere is concerned with content.

The New Age interpretation of whole-brain learning results in the students' acceptance of the holistic (monistic) world view by inducing mystical states of mind. Therefore, as with the subjective science of the New Age, transpersonal or holistic education requires the prerequisite of a religious conversion. This involves subtle methods for the introduction of holistic learning within our schools. According to Ferguson, "The deliberate use of consciousness-expanding techniques in education, only recently well under way, is new in mass schooling."[47] Ferguson quotes Mario Fantini of the state university of New York in his blunt statement that, "The psychology of becoming has to be smuggled into the schools."[48]

Conclusion

Myths are unconcerned with historical accuracy or factual data. They are designed to "impart a feeling of awe for whatever is mysterious and marvelous in life, depicting a universe in which human beings take their place in a much larger scheme."[49] Therefore, the purpose of myths is to inspire belief and restore hope to troubled civilizations.

The fictitious nature of myth is irrelevant to the blind believer. The power of myths is in their ability to restore belief in hope as a means to a more optimistic outlook on life. The symbols of myth "are reflections of the spiritual potentialities of every one of us. Through contemplating these we evoke their powers in our own lives."[50] Myths, then, are essentially placebos for threatened societies or civilizations.

Myth is the very "soul of the New Age." The metamorphosis of modern man through belief in the medicinal power of the placebo (the New Myth) will deliver our planet from extinction. This is the empty message of the New Myth presently confronting our troubled culture.

Notes to Chapter 3

1. K. C. Cole, *Newsweek*, "Master of the Myth," November 14, 1988, p. 60.

2. Ibid., p. 58.

3. Joseph Campbell, *The Power of Myth* (New York: Doubleday, 1988), p. 32.

4. Irving Hexham and Karla Poewe-Hexham, "The Soul of the New Age," *Christianity Today*, September 2, 1988, p. 19.

5. Campbell, *The Power of Myth*, p. 39.

6. Hexham and Poewe-Hexham, "The Soul of the New Age," p. 20.

7. Ibid.

8. Ibid.

9. Among many celebrated contemporary scientists are: Edgar Mitchell, former Apollo 14 astronaut and founder/director of the Institute of Noetic Sciences in Sausalito, California; Dr. Herbert Benson, Harvard University; Dr. Elmer Gree, Menninger Clinic; Dr. Charles Tart and Dr. Fritjof Capra, both of the University of California; Dr. Stanley Krippner, President of the Saybrook Institute; Dr. Dan Goleman, Senior Editor, "Psychology Today"; and Dr. Hal Puthoff, Stanford Research Institute.

10. Quoted in Ferguson, *The Aquarian Conspiracy*, p. 145.

11. Ibid., p. 10.

12. Fritjof Capra, *The Tao of Physics* (New York: Bantam Books, 1983), p. 9.

13. *Webster's New World Dictionary* (New York: Prentice Hall Press, 1984) defines quantum theory as "the theory that energy is not absorbed or radiated continuously but discontinuously, and only in multiples of definite, indivisible units ('quantia')" (p. 1162). The theory of relativity is defined as: " 'Physics' the fact, principle, or theory of the relative, rather than absolute, character of motion, velocity, mass, etc., and the interdependence of matter, time, and space: as developed and mathematically formulated by Albert Einstein and H. A. Lorentz in the special (or restricted) theory of relativity and Einstein in the general theory of relativity" (p. 1198).

14. Ibid., p. 5.

15. Ibid., p. 12.

16. Capra, *The Turning Point*, p. 78.

17. Sharon Fish, "Holistic Health and the Nursing Profession," *SCP Journal*, August 1978, p. 39. This article was adapted by permission by the Spiritual Counterfeits Project from an article in the March 1978 issue of the "The Nurses Lamp" bulletin of Nurses' Christian Fellowship. Copyright 1978 by InterVarsity Christian Fellowship.

18. Dennis Livingston, "Balancing body, mind, and spirit," *The 1988 Guide to New Age Living*, Winter 1988, by Rising Star Associates, Ltd., p. 17.

19. Kenneth Pelletier, *Mind as Healer, Mind as Slayer: A Holistic Approach to Preventing Stress Disorders* (New York: Dell Publishing Co., 1977), p. 195.

20. Ferguson, *The Aquarian Conspiracy*, p. 259.

21. Ibid., p. 260.

22. Ibid., p. 260.
23. Livingston, "Balancing Body, Mind, and Spirit," p. 17.
24. Ibid.
25. Ferguson, *The Aquarian Conspiracy*, p. 277.
26. Dennis Livingston, "Making the personal political," *The 1988 Guide to New Age Living*, p. 34.
27. Fritjof Capra, "National Insecurity," *New Age Journal*, March/April 1988, p. 37.
28. Donald Keys, "All About Planetary Citizens: A Seminar in Four Parts" (transcript), n.d., Seminar III, 1–2. Quoted in Elliot Miller, "Tracking The Aquarian Conspiracy, Part Two," *Christian Research Journal*, Winter/Spring 1987, p. 14.
29. Miller, "Tracking The Aquarian Conspiracy, Part Two," pp. 13–14.
30. Capra, "National Insecurity," p. 41.
31. Ibid.
32. Ibid.
33. See Christine Downing, *The Goddess: Mythological Images of the Feminine* (New York: Crossroad, 1987), chapter 6, "Beginning with Gaia," for an interesting study of the "Great Mother" goddess, Gaia.
34. *Time*, January 2, 1989, p. 2.
35. Miller, "Tracking The Aquarian Conspiracy," p. 10.
36. Ibid.
37. Ferguson, *The Aquarian Conspiracy*, p. 369.
38. Ibid., p. 280.
39. James Howe, *How the Ewoks Saved the Trees. An Old Ewok Legend* (New York: Random House, 1984).
40. Ibid., p. 2.
41. Ibid., p. 30.
42. Ferguson, *The Aquarian Conspiracy*, p. 287.
43. Ibid.
44. Dr. Beverly Galyean, A guided imagery meditation presented at the Confluent Education Workshop, Educ. Workshops, Mandala Conference, San Diego, 4 August 1980. Quoted in: Frances Adeney, "Educators Look East," *SCP Journal*, Winter 1981–82), p. 28.
45. "Radix" interview with Dr. Beverly Galyean by Frances Adeney, 6 August 1980. Also, Dr. Beverly Galyean, "Meditating with Children: Some Things We Learned," "A. P. Newsletter," August–September 1980, p. 16. Contained in "Educators Look East," *SCP Journal*, p. 29.
46. Ferguson, *The Aquarian Conspiracy*, p. 305.
47. Ibid., p. 295.
48. Ibid., p. 281.
49. Donna Rosenberg, *World Mythology, An Anthology of the Great Myths and Epics* (Lincolnwood, Ill.: National Textbook Company, 1986), p. xiv.
50. Campbell, *The Power of Myth*, pp. 217, 218.

4 | *Mythic Themes of the New Age*

The occult odyssey of the New Age entices the spiritual adventurer into a conscious transcending of former categories of duality into the category of oneness, where there is no right or wrong, good or evil; where nothing really is as it seems to be—"Curiouser and curiouser!" This crystalline "separate reality" is inhabited by sorcerers, psychic healers, UFO's, fire-walkers, channelers, goddesses, gurus, fauns, and beckoning spirits which control both nature and the destiny of man. It is a place where eternity intersects with time, an ethereal realm where the spiritual traveler is mystically attuned to an awareness that "The seat of the soul is there where the inner and outer worlds meet."[1]

Shamanism

There is a basic theme running through all myths that originally all was one. Separation—heaven and earth, male and female, light and dark—came about later when the enlightened super races of men plunged into decline, losing their innate psychic powers. The spiritual adventurer experiences a celestial ascent, an ecstatic trance, as he passes through the world of duality and discovers the axis of eternity that enjoins heaven, earth, and the underworld with his soul. This is the unseen world of the shaman.

Carlos Castaneda is a colorful writer who decodes the cryptic metaphors of the New Age through his shamanistic adventures. His many popular books provide the accounts of these spiritual excursions.[2] Castaneda is the disciple of a primitive Mexican shaman, Don Juan.

A Shamanistic Journey

After a ritualistic inhaling of excessive amounts of the drug peyote, the Shaman is ready to initiate his journey. The drugged mind of the Shaman fixates upon a part of nature (such as a tree, a mountain, or the surface of a body of water) until he becomes mesmerized. The external world becomes incoherent, mute to the Shaman as he enters the incorporeal primeval world. The Shaman is beginning to walk an ancient path of remembrance, where many past lives are recalled. The primal world of the Shaman is one of constantly changing "realities," a kaleidoscope of mystic images bombarding the psyche of the sorcerer.

The drug-induced state of mind of the Shaman becomes an isthmus between two estranged worlds, the natural world of phenomena and the primeval "universe next door." Within the mind of the Shaman, all dualistic concepts of light and dark, right and wrong, male and female, etc., bleed together into a stream of perfect unity, complete balance. All is one and all that is is merely an extension of the soul of the Shaman. This is the end of the journey, the axis of eternity, where the microcosm and the macrocosm intersect.

The "new realities" encountered through shamanistic journeys are seen as a primal confirmation to the world view of the New Age. Promising health, power, knowledge, and the ability to solve personal problems through a mystical awareness of the self as the center of the universe, they provide an impetus for the seeker of a new age.

Basic shamanistic themes contain the universal myth of a distant Supreme Deity totally removed from the human situation. Heaven and earth are separated. The role of the shaman "is to serve as charismatic center of a cultist, around which a new symbolic cosmos, and ultimately transformed world (through processes really mystical or apocalyptic rather than historical) will form itself."[3] The spiritual ascent of the shaman brings him into contact with incorporeal entities that are conceived of as intermediaries between heaven and earth. These spiritual entities aid the shaman in his quest to cross over the great chasm between heaven and earth. The shaman then experiences the dissolution of all dualities, the realization of the oneness of all existence. "By gaining admission to the axis of eternity, the shaman also brings supernatural powers to bear in the earthly realm."[4] The image of the axis is critical to the shamanistic world view: "It represents the point at which the natural and supernatural are fused, time is suspended in eternity, and potentiality is full."[5] The axis is the ultimate point of spiritual euphoria in the shamanistic journey. It is the ecstasy of the union of heaven and earth within the being of the shamanistic medium through the agency of other-dimensional spiritual beings.

The predisposition of the New Age to supernatural novelty has also revived the ancient heresy of Gnosticism, another form of spiritual expression from antiquity closely related to shamanism.

Ancient Gnosticism

The word "Gnosticism" comes from the Greek word *gnōsis*, which means "knowledge." This refers not to cognitive or intellectual knowledge, but to a special, revealed knowledge necessary for salvation.

This secret, higher knowledge was available only to an elite. The religion of Gnosticism was not, however, a monolithic system. Gnosticism rather embodied numerous exclusive groups. Although there was great diversity within the whole of Gnosticism, virtually all Gnostics agreed in condemning matter as an evil illusion. The Gnostics did not believe that the supreme God (divine Mind) of pure spirit had anything to do with the illusory physical world. Many of the gnostic systems assigned the creation of the physical world to a lesser god referred to as a Demiurge. The Demiurge is frequently identified as Yahweh, the God of the Old Testament, in gnostic literature.

Harold O. J. Brown notes that, "Gnosticism was a response to the widespread desire to understand the mystery of being: it offered detailed, secret knowledge of the whole order of reality, claiming to know and to be able to explain things of which ordinary, simple Christian faith was entirely ignorant."[6]

The term "Gnosticism" is used with reference to the developed systems of gnostic thought beginning in the second century. Gnosticism was a significant influence between the second and fifth centuries. During this period, Gnosticism was a very formidable opponent of Christian orthodoxy.

Several themes were foundational to gnostic thought. Most outstanding among them was the Redeemer myth. This myth speaks of the preexistence of human souls. The souls of humans were at home in the heavenlies. However, an unknown tragic event took place that resulted in the human souls falling from their heavenly estate to the earth where they became imprisoned within bodies. In this condition, the humans forgot that they had ever enjoyed a former heavenly status. A gnostic Redeemer was sent by the good god to these fallen humans. The mission of the gnostic Redeemer was to bring revelation of their former heavenly estate to the people. This was to be accomplished through the imparting of a special knowledge.

Other versions of this gnostic myth include a Primal Man who is the embodiment of all light. Before the beginning of time, the Primal Man was overcome and destroyed by demonic powers. The evil demons tore the Primal Man into many pieces. Each piece was a separate light particle that the demons used to create a world for themselves out of the chaos of darkness. Some of the light particles were human souls. Because of their imprisonment within fleshly bodies, the demons were able to enslave the humans and make them forget their former heavenly estate. The gnostic Redeemer then came in behalf of the good god to illuminate the captive human souls, through the impartation of a special knowledge, to the realization of their former celestial status. Following their death, these enlightened souls are able to return to the Redeemer.

Because the material world was considered to be the creation of the Demiurge, the good god was separated from the earthly habitat of man by a great expanse. Seven immense spheres of space separated the good god from earth-bound man. These spheres were inhabited by a great host of intermediary beings (often referred to as aeons), who were emanations of the good god. Their role was to assist the gnostic initiate in the reunion of his soul (the particle of divine light) to the transcendent domain of the good god.

Each of the spheres was under the control of a demonic ruler. This demon (often referred to as an Archon, meaning ruler) sought to block the path of the human soul's return to the good god.

By the second century, Jesus Christ was introduced into the gnostic myth as one of the intermediaries. Christ came to earth in order to assist man in his return to the good god. "Christ came into the world, not in order to suffer and die, but in order to release the divine spark of light imprisoned in matter."[7] Jesus Christ was not a savior in the gnostic scheme, "he was a revealer. He came for the express purpose of communicating his secret gnosis."[8] The secret gnosis of the gnostic Christ was the realization of the elite that they too were Christs. The gnostic Jesus was not unique in his office as Christ.

The gnostic could not conceive of Jesus Christ partaking of evil flesh; the incarnation was anathema in their thinking; therefore, he only appeared to be in bodily form. This belief is central to Docetic Gnosticism. Docetism was widely propagated by Marcion, the first great heretic of the Christian Church. The influence of Docetic thought, before it developed into a coherent system in the second century, is evident in the first century by allusions to its principal themes in the epistle of First John.

A radical dualism further characterizes Gnosticism. The many dualistic themes of Gnosticism (the good god and the demon rulers, matter and spirit, the soul and the body, light and dark) are common to all versions of the gnostic myth.

Harold O. J. Brown summarizes: "The gnostic movement has two salient features that appeal to countless minds in every age, i.e., the claim to present a secret lore, explaining otherwise incomprehensible mysteries, and the assertion that its secrets are accessible only to the elite – thus by implication defining as elite all who take an active interest in them."[9] However, the gnostic myth was merely "an elaborate and fanciful structure of doctrines and ideas for which there was no guarantee other than their own imagination."[10]

Neo-Gnosticism

The influence of the gnostic myth upon the New Age is very evident. Popular New Age author and transpersonal psychologist, Ken Wilber writes, "Human life is moving 'up' from Eden, not down. The Fall . . . was nothing less than the involuntary descent of God into matter – the creation of the universe itself. . . . The universe is involved in a mighty drama of awakening and reunion. . . . Salvation [represents] a progression to the transpersonal state – to awareness of our prior union with God."[11]

The New Age is an adulterated form of Gnosticism. The inclusion of other mythic motifs (e.g., UFO's, fascination with Stonehenge, Egyptian pyramids) crowds Gnosticism into a corner of the New Age myth. Yet the gnostic influence is, nonetheless, ever present in New Age thought.

In his search for cosmic consciousness, New Age man often makes contact with so-called spiritual "helpers," "guides," "allies," "guardians," or other spiritual intermediaries. In common with ancient Gnosticism, the New Ager seeks to become intuitively (mystically) aware of his own Christ-consciousness (synonym for cosmic consciousness) through contact with the divine Mind (good god) and by the aid provided by intermediary spiritual beings. David Spangler, a New Age author and lecturer, integrates the gnostic world view into the New Age vision:

> This is the New Age vision: what man is capable of and what man will become because of his own self-initiated efforts in harmony with the aid that he is being given from other sources. A new age dawns upon the Earth. The call goes forth above the clamor and battle sounds of Armageddon, that now there will be peace on Earth and good will flowing between men, for now is the age of the birth of the Christ within the heart of humanity.[12]

A Course in Miracles is a pseudo-gnostic work in three volumes that has gained enthusiastic acceptance within New Age circles. The *Course* was channeled through Helen Schucman by an inner voice. Schucman identifies the inner voice as belonging to Jesus Christ.[13]

The *Course* teaches that God is impersonal oneness, divine Mind. In keeping with the world view of the New Age, God is presented in pantheistic terms. All spiritual paths lead to God.

The *Course* teaches that God created the Son of God. In fact, the only thing God has ever created is the Son of God. This theme contains both the great metaphysical problem of mankind and the good news that humanity so desperately needs to understand.

Echoing the myth of the Primal Man in ancient Gnosticism, the *Course* tells us that somehow the Son of God fell asleep. Although the Son of God possessed the same divine attributes of God, he dreamed that he fell from his role of Creator. In his dream state, the Son denied that God was his creator and asserted that he had created himself. This assertion gave rise to ego and its belief that God is separate from his creation.

God created the Holy Spirit, according to the *Course*, to awaken the Son to the reality of his true identity as Creator. However, the Son of God misunderstood the purpose of the Holy Spirit coming to him, because of his own ego's informing him of his separation from God. The frightened Son fled deeper into his dream and ended in projecting his ego into an illusory physical world. The Son's ego was divided into a multitude of egos, all of which inherited the imagery of separation. The ego, because of separation, conceives of sin, guilt, sickness, and fear. The ego creates a fear of God within us. We fear God because our egos inform us that we have offended him through sin. God, there-fore, desires to judge us and sentence us to a severe punishment.

The *Course* teaches that our fear towards God is unwarranted. Our ego has deluded us into believing that we have sinned against God re-sulting in our separation from him. The *Course* instead instructs us to respond to the call of the Holy Spirit and return to our true identity as sinless emanations of God. When we recognize ourselves, we rec-ognize God, for we are one with him.[14] We are then able to attain complete equality with Jesus, according to the *Course*.[15]

Atonement is the correction of the false belief that we are sinners, as taught by the *Course*. Salvation results from our correction of the ego's illusion of separation. In his insightful article on *A Course in Miracles*, Dean Halverson summarizes the Crucifixion, according to the *Course*, as Jesus' demonstration that "it is possible to declare the truth of our guiltlessness in the midst of the ego's guilt-ridden world. When he was attacked, he chose not to affirm the guilt of his attackers. Only the ego would use an attack to project blame onto others. Instead, Jesus chose to affirm the guiltlessness of his attackers by denying the attack had any effect."[16]

The Jesus of the *Course* reintroduces the mythic motif of a gnos-tic Redeemer by informing humanity of their "true" identity as sinless extensions of God. As Christened beings, in the gnostic tradition, we are able to absolve the guilt of others by refusing to project guilt upon them.[17]

Astrology was important to much of Gnosticism. The Gnostics often turned to the counsel of the stars and planets in seeking means to escape the bondage of their earthly habitation.

Astrology

For many, the idea of the New Age has come to them because of a modern resurgence in the interest of astrology. What is astrology? Basically, astrology contends that the position of the stars and planets at the time of people's birth has a direct influence upon their destiny. Horoscopes thus become a chart depicting someone's life in relation-ship to the heavenly bodies.

Astrologers are predicting the dawning of the Age of Aquarius. The Picean Age (the dispensation aligned with Christianity) is coming to a close, which will place the world in a post–Christian era. *The Aquarian Gospel of Jesus the Christ*, an esoteric version of the teachings of Jesus Christ, forecasts a spiritual age of universal "harmony and understanding":

> The Aquarian Age is preeminently a spiritual age, and the spiritual side of the great lessons that Jesus gave to the world may now be comprehended by multitudes of people, for the many are now coming in an advance stage of spiritual consciousness.[18]

The Age of Aquarius will usher in a new spiritual order that will feature man as "the Herald and Truth of the New Age."[19] The consensus among astrologers for the dawning of the Age of Aquarius is March 21, 2000.[20]

Neo-Paganism

The cosmic consciousness of the New Age is often paganistic. As discussed in chapter three, among many New Agers an earth mother deity replaces a heavenly Father. New Age author Mark Satin is open about the movement's paganism:

> Significantly, among those of us at self-development stages six and seven, religious worship has already begun to rely less on the tradition of the sky god and more on the tradition of the earth goddess. As sociologist Robert Bellah sees it, "The sky religions emphasize the paternal, hierarchical, legalistic and ascetic, whereas the earth tradition emphasizes the maternal, communal, expressive and joyful aspects of existence.[21]

Exemplary of paganism within the New Age is the recently celebrated "Harmonic Convergence." On August 16–17, 1987, thousands of New Age aspirants gathered at various "power points" throughout the world. Locations designated as "power points" by New Age visionaries included Mt. Shasta, California, the Black Hills, South Dakota, Washington's Mt. Rainier, Central Park in Manhattan, the Temples of Delphi in Greece, India's Ganges River, the pyramids of Egypt, Machu Picchu, Peru, and Mt. Fuji in Japan.

The faithful gathered to merge their consciousnesses with the energy emanating from the various power points in the earth, thereby hastening the externalization of the New Age. New Agers sought to synchronize their consciousness with the earthly powers through humming ("vibrational toning," the term applied to this meditative technique).

The harmonious blending of consciousnesses among the more "enlightened" was designed to awaken the rest of the human race to the coming day of global tranquility. This paganistic festival is born out of the New Age's longing for world peace.

Jose Arguelles is the originator of Harmonic Convergence. Arguelles believed that August 16–17, 1987, marked a confluence of astrological and chronological phenomena. Arguelles describes this phenomena as "a turning point of historic magnitude exceeding anything we've ever known."[22] According to Arguelles, the thirteen cycles of heaven and the nine cycles of hell come to an end on the Aztec calendar. The Aztecs believed that the fulfillment of their calendar would eventuate in the second coming of the god Quetzacoatl.

Quetzacoatl is a mythic hero who is to bring peace with him to the earth. The Hopi Indians believed that on August 16, 1987, 144,000 enlightened teachers would awaken the rest of humanity to global peace. Further, it had been 23,412 years (dating from 1987) since the nine planets of our solar system were in perfect alignment. This phenomenon, occurring again on August 16, 1987, was expected to cause a great convulsion of energy within the earth. Finally, the Mayans' "great cycle," which runs from 3113 B.C. to A.D. 2012, came to within 25 years of its termination on August 16 and 17, 1987. Arguelles believed that on August 16–17, 1987, the earth would be in a position to synchronize with the rest of the galaxy, culminating in world peace by A.D. 2012.

Newsweek asked Carl Raschke of the University of Denver to explain the Harmonic Convergence. Raschke states the obvious, "That's the case with just about all New Age beliefs, . . . They're ad-libbed to fit the occasion."[23]

The World Peace Event has become an annual happening among New Age peace activists. A flyer advertising the World Peace Event on December 31, 1986, to take place at the Kingdome in Seattle, Washington (one location among many international locales), stated that at noon, Greenwich time (4:00 A.M. Pacific Standard Time), 500,000,000 people would join together for one hour of meditation for world peace. According to the flyer, 42 countries, including the Soviet Union, and 57 U.S. cities, would participate in this peace vigil.

The spiritually intoxicating New Age-type music filled Seattle's Kingdome as people participated in guided visualization for planetary unity amidst the eerie wolf howls of other pagans for peace. Unfortunately for these peace-loving pagans, reports following this first World Peace Event indicated that the New Age fell far short of the hoped for 500,000,000 worldwide participants.

Evolution

Instead of gradualism, the evolutionary model of the New Myth is scientifically referred to as *punctuated equilibrium*. Rather than a gradual monolithic evolution of the universe and living species, punctuated equilibrium postulates periodic, isolated leaps by small groups of species. Marilyn Ferguson comments on the theory of punctuated equilibrium as it is reinterpreted within the context of the New Age paradigm:

> This changing view is significant for at least two reasons: (1) It requires a mechanism for biological change more powerful than chance mutation, and (2) it opens us up to the possibility of rapid evolution in our own time, when the equilibrium of the species is punctuated by stress. Stress in modern society is experienced at the frontiers of our psychological rather than our geographical limits. Pioneering becomes an increasingly psychospiritual venture since our physical frontiers are all but exhausted, short of space exploration.[24]

Conscious evolution resulting in the deification of man is the primary mythic motif of the New Age. Psychologist Barry McWaters defines conscious evolution from a New Age perspective: "Conscious evolution" is that latter phase in evolutionary process wherein the developing entity becomes conscious of itself, aware of the process in which it is involved and begins voluntarily to participate in the work of evolution.[25] The evolutionary myth, specifically as it is used in support of the concept of conscious evolution, is the quintessential component of New Age ideology.

Stanford Research International is a think tank in search of the new mythic hero. In a report entitled, *Changing Images of Man*, SRI redefined human nature and potential in a prescriptive fashion as follows:

We have attempted in this study to:

> 1. Illuminate ways our present society, its citizens, and institutions have been shaped by the underlying myths and images of the past and present.
>
> 2. Explore the deficiencies of currently held images of humankind and to identify needed characteristics of future images.

3. Identify high-leverage activities that could facilitate the emergence of new images and new policy approaches to the resolution of key problems in society.[26]

SRI concludes in recommending that the new image of man be understood in infinite terms. Quoting from the Upanishads (Hindu sacred writings), SRI presents its ideal human image:

The atma, the Self, is never born and never dies.

It is without cause and is eternally changeless.

It is beyond time, unborn, permanent, and eternal.

It does not die when the body does.

Concealed in the heart of all beings lies the atma, the Spirit, the Self;

Smaller than the smallest atom, greater than the greatest spaces.[27]

In his essay, "The Funeral of a Great Myth," C. S. Lewis astutely observed that "the scientific theory deals with development, while the myth deals with improvements."[28] Hexham and Poewe-Hexham further state that "New Age myths need not be systematic or logically connected, provided they can tie into the grand myth of evolution and so become supporting elements in a greater whole."[29]

Conclusion

These mythic threads run throughout the whole of New Age thought from politics to holistic health food centers. The mythic themes of the New Age inform its adherents of values critical to the realization of its grand vision. Perhaps the supreme value emphasized within the New Age is survival. The struggle for survival is foundational to both evolutionary theories, either punctuationist or Darwinian gradualism.

The "grand myth" of evolution drives the New Age in its commitment to issues involving planetary and racial survival such as ecological concerns, the nuclear arms race, human rights violations, starvation, overpopulation, and political tensions. The New Age is committed to a planetary paradise ("planetization") through its abiding trust in the unlimited potentialities of the human species. Accelerating the evolutionary process within the human species through the administration of the various psychospiritual technologies available within the Movement will, according to New Age enthusiasts, insure global and racial survival. The mythic themes further inform the New Age advocate of the underlying interconnectedness of all reality. Ancient myths resurfacing in the New Age appear to validate its monistic world view, that all is One. The notion of mankind's ascent to godhood is drawn from his sense of oneness with all reality. Man then becomes the persona of the impersonal god of pantheism that imbues all of reality.

Since all of reality is interconnected, according to the New Age world view, then every individual entity affects the whole. A true sense of oneness then is integral to the ultimate socio-political vision of a unified planetary system. The concept of interconnectedness provides the ethical basis for this unprecedented magnitude of global cooperation.

The value of non-violence grows out of the New Age's emphasis upon survival and interconnectedness. Violence results in separation, the greatest evil in New Age thought, for it is counterproductive to its highest ideals.

Borrowing from Taoism, the New Age is devoted to the metaphysical concept of balance (the concept of yin and yang) between the microcosm (man) and the macrocosm (the universe). Proper balance creates the sense of perfect unity, contrary to the notion of separation, with the "universal life energy." New Age spiritual technologies serve to induce the sense of metaphysical balance centered in the human heart.

Human autonomy transcends all previous humanistic notions of the term in the New Age, taking on cosmic proportions. The mythic themes of the New Age inform the spiritual adventurer that there is no greater power beyond his own consciousness. The Self is ultimate reality as expressed by Shirley MacLaine: "We already know everything. The knowingness of our divinity is the highest intelligence."[30] Celebrated guru Swami Muktananda also echos the mythic motifs of the New Age: "Kneel to your own self. Honor and worship your own being. God dwells in you as you."[31]

Notes to Chapter 4

1. Campbell, *The Power of Myth*, p. 57.
2. For an account of a shamanistic journey through the eyes of the popular fiction author Carlos Castaneda, see *A Separate Reality* (New York: Pocket Books, 1971), pp. 171–74.

3. Robert S. Ellwood and Harry B. Partin, *Religious and Spiritual Groups in Modern America* (Englewood Cliffs, N.J.: Prentice-Hall, 1988), pp. 13–14.

4. Brooks Alexander, "A Generation of Wizards: Shamanism & Contemporary Culture," *Spiritual Counterfeits Project*, Special Collection Journal, Winter 1984, vol. 6, no. 1, p. 26.

5. Ibid.

6. Harold O. J. Brown, *Heresies* (New York: Doubleday, 1984), p. 39.

7. Ibid., p. 222.

8. Ibid.

9. Ibid., p. 44.

10. Ibid.

11. Quoted in Christopher Lasch, "Soul of a New Age," *Omni*, October 1987, p. 85.

12. Spangler, *Revelation: The Birth of a New Age*, p. 149.

13. *A Course in Miracles, vol. 3, Manual for Teachers* (Tiburon, Calif.: Foundation for Inner Peace, 1985), p. 56.

14. Ibid., vol. 1, p. 136.

15. Ibid., p. 5.

16. Dean C. Halverson, "A Course in Miracles, Seeing Yourself as Sinless," *SCP Journal*, vol. 7, no. 1, 1987, p. 22.

17. *A Course in Miracles*, vol. 1, p. 415.

18. Levi Dowling, *The Aquarian Gospel of Jesus the Christ* (Marina del Rey: De Vorss & Co., 1964), pp. 10–11.

19. Spangler, *Revelation: The Birth of a New Age*, p. 105.

20. John Weldon and Clifford Wilson, *Occult Shock and Psychic Forces* (San Diego: Master, 1980), p. 111.

21. Mark Satin, *New Age Politics* (New York: Dell Publishing Co., 1978), p. 114.

22. Bill Barol and Pamela Abramson, "The End of the World (Again)," *Newsweek*, August 17, 1987, p. 70.

23. Ibid., p. 71.

24. Ferguson, *The Aquarian Conspiracy*, p. 159.

25. Barry McWaters, *Conscious Evolution* (Los Angeles: New Age Press, 1981), pp. 27–28.

26. O. W. Markley and Willis W. Harman, eds., *Changing Images of Man* (New York: Pergamon Press, 1982), p. xxii. Quoted in Alexander, "Occult Philosophy and Mystical Experience," p. 14.

27. Ibid., p. 135; p. 14 in Alexander, "Occult Philosophy and Mystical Experience."

28. Quoted in Hexham and Poewe-Hexham, "The Soul of the New Age," p. 21.

29. Ibid.

30. Minnery, "Unplugging the New Age," p. 2.

31. Ibid.

5 | *Critiquing the New Age Myth*

Whereas the New Age must be commended for its apparent humanitarian concerns of racial and planetary preservation, are its Eastern occultic means able to deliver a global paradise? In other words, is the New Age a grand apocalyptic solution?

Harold Lindsell, editor emeritus of *Christianity Today*, sets forth the two most basic, yet important questions in life: (1) "Where do I go for answers to life's most important questions?" and (2) "Is my source reliable?"[1] With this challenge in mind, we will now determine if the New Age does in fact provide reliable, substantiated answers for the present human malady.

Holism: A New Scientific Paradigm

The interconnectedness of all the systems of the universe, inclusive of man, is an axiom of New Age ideology. This concept, according to its proponents, is bedrock for the hope of a New Age. In seeking to integrate their ideology within the mainstream of Western thought, New Agers, such as Fritjof Capra, are endeavoring to wed science with Eastern mysticism:

> Thus, the awareness of the profound harmony between the world view of modern physics and the views of Eastern mysticism now appears as an integral part of a much larger cultural transformation, leading to the

emergence of a new vision of reality that will require a fundamental change in our thoughts, perceptions, and values. . . . From this point of view, the connection between physics and mysticism is not only very interesting but also extremely important. It shows that the results of modern physics have opened up two very different paths for scientists to pursue. They may lead us – to put it in extreme terms – to the Buddha or to the Bomb, and it is up to each scientist to decide which path to take. It seems to me that at a time when close to half of our scientists and engineers work for the military, wasting an enormous potential of human ingenuity and creativity by developing ever more sophisticated means of total destruction, the path of the Buddha, the "path with a heart," cannot be overemphasized.[2]

The mechanistic scientific model (Cartesian-Newtonian) is the focus of Capra's indictment. Fragmentation, resulting from an overemphasis upon rationality, has created untold problems within the planetary culture, according to proponents of the new science.

Chapter two of this book demonstrated how eighteenth-century thought (the Enlightenment) gave rise to the rationalism and determinism that came to be dominant in Western thought. The extreme caricature of the Cartesian model, resulting from the rationalism and determinism of atheistic humanism, has been reductionistic to both scientific inquiry and human dignity. On this point, the Christian Church and the New Age shake hands. The Church should avoid an apologetic of such excessive reductionism. However, is the solution the opposite extreme? Have we really come down to a choice between "Buddha or the Bomb?" Is our only means of survival to flee to the shrine of holistic thought, to consecrate ourselves to a world view of the interconnectedness of the systems of the universe, in effect, embrace Eastern monism?

The issue at stake in this great debate is addressed by researcher Elliot Miller: "What is the primary 'cause' underlying the many symptoms of our global 'disease'?"[3] Mark Davidson, a science writer quoted by Miller, is in essential agreement with Capra, "the fault, . . . is not in our stars and not entirely in ourselves – but substantially in our systems."[4] Disagreeing with Davidson, Miller strikes at the heart of the issue: "To place the blame primarily on our systems rather than ourselves is to diagnose a symptom of the disease as its cause."[5]

Rather than withdrawing further into the depths of his own moral depravity through intuitive development, man needs a thorough change of heart. The New Age ignores the reality of man's sinful nature. By placing human consciousness on the throne of the universe, through the assumption of human perfectness, New Age man is actually glorifying the source of the human predicament. "The breakdown of the family, its resulting injury to our young, and the spiraling statistics for such social ills as violent crime, drug and alcohol abuse, and sexually transmitted diseases are ultimately the results of sin, not faulty systems."[6]

Ian Barbour, a noted authority on the relation between science and philosophy/theology, allows us to probe deeper in our evaluation of the new science by asking two penetrating questions:

> For what reason do we reject the mechanistic world-view that once claimed support from classical physics: (a) was the mistake a "scientific" one, which we now reject because of new scientific discoveries, or (b) was it a "philosophical" and "epistemological" mistake involving an uncritical transition from physics to metaphysics? In the second case we would conclude that a mechanistic world-view never did have legitimate justification, even when it claimed to be based on the best science of its day; and the lesson from the past would lead us to be wary today about extending modern physics into a new metaphysics.[7]

The "uncritical transition from physics to metaphysics" is characteristic of proponents of the subjective science of the New Myth. Former Apollo 14 astronaut Edgar Mitchell is a very visible advocate of the new subjective science. In a *New Age Journal* interview, Mitchell stated that "I have experimented with virtually all of these techniques—gestalt therapy, rolfing, Scientology, psychological processing with different professionals—all trying to research and understand this process of how you get yourself consistent. How do you get your conscious awareness and your subconscious awareness working in harmony with each other?"[8]

The subjective science of the New Age views the universe as one inseparable reality (monism). A religious conversion must precede this perception of the universe as one organic whole. This results in the observer merely being an extension of his own observations. Therefore, "scientific" observations by proponents of the new science are so muddied by mysticism that the result is a complete departure from critical objective analysis, characteristic of the classic scientific method. "To put it another way, we have a group of scientists who say that the universe *seems* to be made up of the same cosmic 'stuff' according to the *theories* of *some* theoretical physicists, who in turn have interpreted the data by *their* belief systems. All things considered, it just doesn't wash."[9]

The critical role of belief, as an integral part of "scientific" investigation, is further illustrated in Capra's *The Tao of Physics* as he attempts to conform Einstein's unified field theory to his own monistic world view:

In recent years, there has been an increasing amount of evidence that the protons and neutrons, too, are composite objects; but the forces holding them together are so strong or—what amounts to the same—the velocities acquired by the components are so high, that the *relativistic picture* (my italics) has to be applied where the forces are also particles. Thus the distinction between the constituent particles and the particles making up the binding forces becomes *blurred* (my italics) and the approximation of an object consisting of constituent parts breaks down. The particle world cannot be decomposed into elementary components.[10]

Capra is guilty of a non sequitur (a logical fallacy). The conclusion that he draws concerning the scientific inability to decompose the particle world into "elementary components" does not follow from his premise, wherein he speaks of the difficulty in distinguishing between constituent particles and those particles that make up the binding forces within nature.

It is at this point that Capra, and many other advocates of the subjective science of the New Myth, is guilty of yet another logical fallacy, circular reasoning. Capra overcomes the "blurred" distinction between the constituent particles and the particles that make up the "binding forces" through his own application of the "relativistic picture," a mystical state of mind. The proponents of the new science set out to prove what they have already accepted as fact because of their prior conversion to a monistic-pantheistic world view induced by Eastern mysticism.

Through appeal to Einstein's unified field theory, there is absolutely no reason to reject the biblical account of creation. The Bible teaches that a single source is responsible for the existence of the universe. Metaphysical realities cannot be finally concluded by scientific inquiry. "This being the case, it is clear that whatever evidence exists for the unity of the *physical* universe, it does not constitute support for *metaphysical* monism."[11] Therefore, "it becomes clear that Dr. Capra is not reasoning from premise to conclusion. He is not proposing a theory but announcing a revelation."[12] This introduces a grave problem—the subjective revelations of Capra and others are unverifiable leaps in the dark. These men have departed from science altogether. The new science is not science at all, it is religion. Dr. Jack Sarfatti, director of the San Francisco-based Physics/Consciousness Research Group, boldly states, "We want to infect society with a different view of reality. Physicists are the high priests of society."[13]

Stanford University's Richard Bube provides us with a timely observation concerning the new subjective science by concluding that "the

choice of religious implication [is] derived from quite nonscientific in-
puts and not impelled by the scientific model at all."[14]

Pan-Evolution

Pan-evolutionism is foundational to the New Myth. Evolution
is comprehensive of the cosmological, biological, sociopolitical, and
psychospiritual development of mankind. Evolution will result in the
new planetary order, according to New Age hopefuls. In its preemi-
nence in New Age ideology, evolution is a sacrament to believers in
the cosmic ascendancy of mankind. Conscious evolution is to the New
Age what the Resurrection is to Christianity.

As discussed in chapter four, the evolutionary model of the New
Myth is punctuated equilibrium, instead of Darwinian gradualism. It
is helpful to repeat, in part, Marilyn Ferguson's understanding of punctuated equilibrium and its perceived effects on the human consciousness as part of my evaluation of the New Age paradigm:

> The new paradigm attributes evolution to periodic leaps by small groups.
> This changing view is significant for at least two reasons: (1) It requires
> a mechanism for biological change more powerful than chance mutation,
> and (2) it opens us up to the possibility of rapid evolution in our own
> time, when the equilibrium of the species is punctuated by stress. Stress
> in modern society is experienced at the frontiers of our psychological
> rather than our geographical limits.[15]

Is there a known, scientifically valid, mechanism to account for
the beginning and perpetual increasing organization of the universe?
An inductive examination of four logical possibilities for the origin of
the universe will answer this question.[16] The first explanation argues
that the universe isn't there at all; it is an illusion. This is the view of
the universe held by Eastern mysticism. The universe is ordered by our
own imagination, or as far as we know, our galaxy burned out eons
of time ago and what we have now is only a small picture of just our
solar system.

Scientifically, several problems exist with this explanation. For
example, colors are universal. Stop lights govern people universally, a
point that demonstrates objective reality instead of the concept of reality
as being the projection of our individual minds. The whole world obeys
outward stimuli. Further, empirical verification demonstrates that reality

transcends our own minds. Scientifically, light reflections are measurable (in a red spectrum); the speed of the earth's rotation can be measured as well. Solar-lunar eclipses can be predicted. Illusions can be neither measured or predicted.

The next second and third explanations concern either punctuated equilibrium or gradualism. The first, spontaneous generation, contends that the universe spontaneously arose out of nothing. Scientifically, this view fails as well. A basic axiom of physics posits that from nothing, nothing comes forth. This is an absurd impossibility. Impersonal matter, or consciousness, does not produce life or personality. Scientists Spallanzani, Redi, and Pasteur conclusively proved that all life arises from preexisting life.[17] Miller further notes that, "Systems theorists offer us no explanation as to how inorganic parts brought into complex relationship could possibly produce 'life,' or how organic parts brought into complex relationship could possibly produce 'mind' (let alone the human psyche). They just assure us that they do."[18]

Louis Pasteur, in demonstration that micro-organisms could not be spontaneously generated, said "the resultant recognition that micro-organisms, like all the more visible forms of life, are reproduced only by their own kind, made possible the establishment of bacteriology as a precise science, and its revolutionary application in immunology and in the treatment of infectious disease."[19] Pasteur's notable scientific discoveries were in agreement with the Bible, that things reproduce only "after their own kind" (Genesis 1:11, 21, 24, 25).

The second of these two explanations, and third overall, is the belief that the universe always was. The late Sir Fred Hoyle, an astronomer and cosmologist, is the author of this theory. The Fred Hoyle Theory is also known as the Steady-State Theory. This theory argues that the universe expands and contracts from infinity to infinity, continually expanding out and in.

The Second Law of Thermodynamics demonstrates that all energy tends to maximum entropy (referred to as Absolute Zero in the scientific community). This is known as the principle of decay. The Second Law of Thermodynamics further demonstrates that entropy increases with time as order in the universe is transformed to disorder. This stands in direct contradiction to the evolutionary model, gradual and punctuated equilibrium. Dr. Don N. Page, physics professor at Pennsylvania State University, delivers the death blow to both gradualism or punctuated equilibrium by stating that "The mystery is not that an ordered state should become disordered but that the early universe was in a highly ordered state."[20] Page further states that "There is no mechanism known as yet that would allow the universe to begin in an arbitrary state and then evolve to its present highly ordered state."[21] In an effort to counter the overwhelming evidence against their claims of punctuated equilibrium, New Agers have advanced a law that supposedly stabilizes the effects of the Second Law of Thermodynamics. New Agers argue for the law of "syntropy" (introduced in chapter one).

Although New Agers acknowledge the Second Law of Thermodynamics, they must explain the existence of highly ordered systems. Presupposing evolution, New Agers then accept the invention (contrary to scientific discovery) of the law of syntropy in order to explain the highly organized systems of the universe. Miller again cites the fallacy in New Age reasoning: "Here New Agers and systems thinkers are guilty of question-begging. Why consider evolution a fact? Why postulate an unproven law (syntropy) to counteract a demonstrable law (entropy) in order to keep one model, when another model fits the facts of science as we find them?"[22]

Dr. Henry M. Morris, of the Institute for Creation Research, further notes that the observation of an irreversible entropy in the universe indicates that "vertical" evolution toward higher levels of complexity is not even possible.[23] Thus, their exists no scientific evidence that evolution occurred in the past or is occurring in the present.

Pantheistic notions are yet further vain attempts to explain the existence of the universe. Morris logically asserts that "In fact, polytheism in practice is usually merely the popular expression of pantheism, which identifies God with the universe, and is experienced primarily as animism. A god who is essentially synonymous with the universe and its varied components could never be the cause of the universe."[24]

Conscious evolution is based on the model of punctuated equilibrium. Citing further evidence against punctuated equilibrium, thus destroying the very foundation upon which notions of conscious evolution rests, Miller notes that several evolutionary geneticists and biologists alike consider the model to be fantasy, emphasizing that "so many other delicate systems would be set awry as a result [of such a major change in structure] that the organism could not survive."[25] This concept, if it were true, would have meant Gaia's demise!

The New Age belief in conscious evolution is founded upon another logical fallacy known as equivocation. Equivocation results when the evidence used to support one meaning of a word (in this case evolution) is unwittingly applied as support for an entirely different meaning of the word. In other words, there is absolutely no connection between biological evolution and conscious evolution.

Most people find it very difficult to believe in the evolution of mankind over millions of years. The inclusion of myths about the super races associated with Stonehenge, Atlantis, Machu Picchu, Egyptian pyramids, and extraterrestrials encourage a blind faith in the accelerated evolution of mankind. Hexham and Poewe-Hexham comment that, "At the same time, an eschatological element is introduced: If space people originated life on Earth, surely they must have continued to guide its development. That means we are not alone. And however threatening our situation is in the final analysis, our creators are going to intervene to save us."[26]

John Keel, a parapsychological researcher and author, comments that the superstitions of modern man have "catapulted us backward into realms of knowledge known and practiced by yogis and mystics for thousands of years. We are simply putting respectable scientific labels on old cultist pursuits. Before the end of this century some laconic college professor will probably receive the Nobel Prize for rediscovering principles of science that literally controlled all ancient cultures."[27]

In the face of belief in evolution, Morris concludes that "There is not a single fact of science or history or human experience which cannot be better explained in terms of a primeval creation than a continuing evolution."[28] If none of the complex systems in the world have evolved by natural processes, they must have been created by supernatural processes.

The fourth possible explanation for the existence of the universe is that it was created by a transcendent source greater than itself. We live in a contingent universe (a universe with a beginning). Therefore, there must be another dimensional source eternal in nature, or how else did a contingent universe come into existence? J. Oliver Buswell observes that "If something exists, then something must be eternal, unless something came from nothing."[29]

Albert Einstein demonstrated that we live in an elliptical universe (a contained universe). This conclusion was drawn from his theory of the unity of all fields (unified field theory mentioned above). Our universe then has dimensions and is encompassed, as Einstein speculated, by another universe that dwarfs ours![30] For an unlimited force of energy to hold and contain the universe together in which we live, that power would have to be eternal, omnipotent, and omnipresent.

If the universe demonstrates purpose, order, and design, therein pointing to a personal Creator, it would be reasonable for us to inquire if the Creator of the universe has ever revealed himself to mankind. We will consider the revelation of God to man in chapter six.

Ethics/Pantheism

Arriving at her suite in Philadelphia's Four Seasons Hotel, Shirley MacLaine is disturbingly made aware that she has lost her passport. "Why did I program the loss? That's what I want to know," sighs the actress.[31] One may wonder that if Shirley MacLaine was able to program the loss of her passport, maybe she could reprogram its return. To this reasonable thought, MacLaine responded in the typically irrational terms of the New Age's occult spirituality, "That's probably why I was up all night, trying to get in touch with it, . . . I see it somewhere out there in a plastic bag, but I don't know the location."[32]

Ethics in the New Age are not based upon the character of a holy, transcendent God, as in the case of Judeo-Christianity, but rather New Agers choose to create their own reality.

Our problem is not a sinful condition, but rather the ignorance of our true divine nature. As the god of our own universe, we program our lives to include even our birthplace and choice of parents. This leads to the conclusion drawn by Lifespring, a popular New Age human potential cult, that "We are perfect exactly the way we are. And when we accept that, life works."[33] Therefore, if we experience problems in life, it is because we have imposed those things upon ourselves. The Christian should readily acknowledge that this is half true. We do create many of our own problems in life, for which we must cope with in a mature and responsible manner. However, the Judeo-Christian world view does not reject the reality of external experiences (good or bad) over which we have no control as does the New Age world view.

Werner Erhard, founder of the Forum (formerly est, Erhard Seminars Training), another popular New Age psychospiritual cult, expresses his philosophy of life through the revelation of the self.

> The Self itself is the ground of all being, that from which everything arises[34] . . . when I get in touch with myself and get in touch with yourself, we will see the same self.[35] Self is all there is. I mean that's it.[36]

The extreme narcissism of the Forum, representative of New Age thought from Shirley MacLaine to Fritjof Capra, draws many people who believe that the New Age offers them something that the Church is unable to offer, an emancipated ME!

The late Walter Martin, former director of the Christian Research Institute in Southern California, explains the world view of est (the Forum):

> The estian world view is relativistic, subjective, and self-centered. There is no objective reality or truth; all ethics (issues of right and wrong) are personal and are not submitted to some independent criterion of right and truth; the self becomes the ultimate creator, experiencer, and judge of reality.[37]

Werner Erhard further describes his own world view:

> You believe that reality is something objective, external, existing in its own right. You also believe that the nature of reality is self-evident. When you delude yourself into thinking you see something, you assume that everyone else sees the same thing as you. But I tell you, Winston, that reality is not external. Reality exists in the human mind, and nowhere else.[38]

This world view leads individuals to the conclusion that they are the center and embodiment of the universe. Since reality exists only within the human mind, then we create our own universe and circumstances. The conclusions drawn from this sinister world view were documented by a trainee at one of Erhard's training sessions:

> Snapping back to the present, I heard Werner screaming that we create everything that happens to us in our lives. . . . He said that Vietnamese babies created the napalm that fell on their heads, the Jews constructed Auschwitz, that rape victims desired to be raped. The audience went crazy, screaming, turning off, throwing up their hands in outrage. Werner ran around the room arguing his theory of self-responsibility with each person, obviously trying to offend, shock, scare, create a mood.[39]

The amoral world view of the New Age is at the mercy of man's sinful atrocities. It is without a transcendent point of reference necessary to address basic issues of human rights. In response to an allegation similar to this, Erhard responded, "So est is evil, what's the point? Yea, I got that, now what? So what?"[40] Erhard's indifference grows out of his pantheistic convictions that man is not a sinner by nature, but rather, "My self is absolute."[41]

However, if evil is unreal, as the pantheist would assert, then what is the origin of the illusion of evil? Or, as Norman Geisler asks, "more seriously, how can evil arise from God who is absolutely and necessarily good?"[42] If all is one and man is part of the one, then the presence of evil and suffering in the world must mean that man is inherently sinful.

The pantheist asserts that God is beyond categories of good and evil. However, this results in the inability to distinguish between good and evil, plunging man into the fathomless depths of unrestrained human depravity.

Astrology

Although many New Agers advance the idea that the New Age is here now and we must learn to externalize it through self-discovery, astrologers generally predict that its discovery will dawn March 21, 2000.[43] Astronomers deny any scientific basis for the occult practice of astrology.

Since the basic assumptions of astrology are founded upon a false scientific model, it follows that any conclusions drawn by astrology would also be patently false. Further, astrology is fatalistic. If life is predetermined by the stars, then astrologers are without any objective basis necessary to explain our own world. Contrary to astrology, the Christian world view offers objectivity and therein a means to observe the nature of our universe. Jesus Christ has come from outside of the system in order to reveal to us the nature of our world.

Astrologers overlook the fact that stars are finite. Additionally, the movement of stars results in their positions continually being altered. Stars are not, therefore, eternal, unchanging standards upon which to place trust for the future.

Astrology does not promote the belief that some people can be "born losers," which would be consistent with their assumptions. In other words, if one accepts the basic premise that from birth, our lives are predetermined by the heavenly constellations, then some people would be born under favorable conditions as "born winners" but others are just as likely to be "born losers."

In antiquity, Neptune and Pluto were unknown. Therefore, astrological charts were based only upon the seven planets observable with the naked eye. Since, according to astrology, the position of the planets affect human behavior and earthly events, these two planets should have been charted by astrologers. However, these planets are usually ignored by astrologers. No accurate horoscope could be charted without the inclusion of all of the planets and their alleged influence.[44]

The birth of twins results in yet another problem for the occult science of astrology. Since twins are born at exactly the same time, under the same sign, they should lead identical lives. Human experience, of course, demonstrates that this simply is not the case.

Astrology originated within latitudes relatively close to the equator. As a result, no provisions were made for the higher latitudes where a planet may not be in sight for several weeks in a row.[45] Problems occurring from this short-sightedness are identified by Josh McDowell and Don Stewart:

> This means those living in the higher latitudes in places such as Alaska, Norway, Finland and Greenland have no planetary influence in their lives, for it is almost impossible to calculate what point of the zodiac is rising on the horizon above the Arctic circle.[46]

The faulty premises of astrology result in numerous inaccuracies; however, few astrological failures are more serious, at least to those who are anticipating the golden age of mankind's supreme reign by the year 2000, than the problem cited by Owen S. Rachleff:

> Astronomers at the Hayden Planetarium have poured cold water over the imminence of the Aquarian millennium. According to their conclusive calculations, the so-called age of Aquarius will not dawn until around A.D. 2570.[47]

The spiritual delusion of the astral religion of the original astrologers has come into prominence in the New Age. The Tower of Babel (Genesis 11) was a primal attempt by fallen man to pretentiously ascend to godhood through human effort. The pagan mythology of Babel has resurfaced in the New Age. The spiritual inebriation used in the divine judgment of their ancestors is likely to plunge the New Age into the same heady state of drunken confusion.

Conclusion: The Repackaging of the Primal Lie

Adorned in the optimistic praises of unlimited human potential, the ancient but ever-appealing lie of the Serpent has been reintroduced in the New Age. The mythic themes of the New Age echo the "hidden wisdom" of the primal temptation.

Rather than critically explaining reality, the Eastern occult world view is a philosophical explanation of mystical experience. Beginning with man, the Eastern mystical explanation for the universe is ultimately understood in terms of a cosmic humanism. In other words, man is the center and source of the universe. This interpretation of mystical experience leads man into a monistic description of reality, all is one. The human consciousness connects the macrocosm (the universe) with the microcosm (man) resulting in the personalization of pantheism's impersonal god in man. This vision of wholeness seduces man into believing in his own inherent divinity, the goal of the satanic lie, "ye shall be as gods" (Genesis 3:5).

New Age "prophet" and author David Spangler astoundingly agrees with the Luciferic authoring of the New Age world view. "Lucifer works within each of us to bring us to wholeness, and as we move into a new age, which is the age of man's wholeness, each of us in some way is brought to that point which I term the Luciferic initiation."[48]

The confusion of the Creator with creation (pantheism) ultimately provokes divine judgment (Romans 1:18, 25). In his search for "cosmic totality," New Age man ventures into the secret recesses of the human heart. Through the use of Eastern meditative techniques, New Age man finds that he is the reflection of God's glory. However, instead of glorifying the Lord God in whose image he is created, in his falleness, New Age man chooses to worship the image. This idolatrous tendency of the human condition results in a confusion of the image of God within man with the reality of creation. Brooks Alexander provides astute insight regarding the evil snares of half-truths: "Indeed, without some appearance of reality, the serpent's promise would not have the seductive power that it does. The tragic paradox of our human condition gives this shimmering description much of its verisimilitude: our created nature enables us to reflect the glory of God in a dependent and finite form, but our fallen nature impels us to appropriate the glory of God in an autonomous and infinite form."[49]

Demonic entities, masquerading as Atlantean warriors, revealers of ancient, esoteric wisdom, "ascended masters," "guides," "allies," and "guardians" mimic the same threefold lie of their Master, deluding the minds of the unwary; divine wisdom is a possession of man's inner being, death is not real, and man is a god (Genesis 3:1–5). This threefold lie is injected into the human psyche through its gnostic promise of spiritual illumination. Through the manipulation of spiritual laws, the neo-gnostic of the New Age becomes the creator and controller of his own reality. Contrary to empirical evidence, the neo-gnostics of the New Age go "out on a limb" and attempt to erect an elaborate belief system for which there is no foundation other than their own fallen imagination.

Popular New Age writer Dick Sutphen is the editor of *Master of Life* magazine. Sutphen inadvertently lays an ax to his own limb in his response to a "metaphysically disabled" New Ager wearied in her multi-tangent quest after "Christ consciousness" by stating that " 'Foo-foos' are those hiding from reality in groundless beliefs."[50] The New Age is founded upon extremely unreliable sources and as a result, to trust in this pernicious fable as a solution for the sociopolitical ills of our planet is to prescribe a cure that is ultimately worse than the disease.

Notes to Chapter 5

1. Dr. Harold Lindsell sets forth this challenge as a part of his address to new students at the Fall, 1984, orientation at The Simon Greenleaf School of Law, Anaheim, California.

2. Capra, *The Tao of Physics*, p. xvii.

3. Elliot Miller, "The New Myth, A Critique of New Age Ideology," *Forward*, Spring–Summer 1986, p. 25.

4. Mark Davidson, *Uncommon Sense* (Los Angeles: J. P. Tarcher, Inc., 1983), p. 159. Quoted in Miller, "The New Myth, A Critique of New Age Ideology," p. 25.

5. Ibid.

6. Ibid.

7. Ian G. Barbour, *Issues in Science and Religion* (New York: Harper Torchbooks, 1971), 289. Quoted in Miller, "The New Myth, A Critique of New Age Ideology," p. 26.

8. Florence Graves, "Ultimate Frontier," *New Age Journal*, May/June 1988, p. 52.

9. Mark Albrecht and Brooks Alexander, "The Sellout of Science," *SCP Journal*, August 1978, p. 26.

10. Capra, *The Tao of Physics*, p. 70.

11. Albrecht and Alexander, "The Sellout of Science," p. 26.

12. Ibid.

13. Rasa Gustaitis, "Faster Than a Speeding Photon," *City of San Francisco*, 7 October 1975, p. 23. Quoted in Albrecht and Alexander, "The Sellout of Science," p. 24.

14. Richard Bube, "Pseudo-Science and Pseudo-Theology: Cosmic Consciousness," *Journal of the American Scientific Affiliation* 29, no. 4 (December, 1977), p. 170. Quoted in Albrecht and Alexander, "The Sellout of Science," p. 26.

15. Ferguson, *The Aquarian Conspiracy*, p. 159.

16. There exist numerous theories as explanation for the origin of the universe. However, these many theories are reducible to the four set forth here

and in chapter 6. These four explanations for the origin of the universe were advanced by Dr. Frank Allen, chairman of the physics department, University of Manitoba. These four possibilities were a part of a lecture given by Dr. Walter R. Martin, Fall Semester, 1984, at the Simon Greenleaf School of Law, Anaheim, California.

17. Thomas A. Easton and Carl E. Rischee, *Bioscope* (New York: Charles E. Merrill Publishers, 1984), pp. 13–14.

18. Miller, "The New Myth: A Critique of New Age Ideology," p. 26.

19. Aram Vartanian, *Dictionary of the History of Ideas*, vol. 4 (New York: Charles Scribner's Sons, 1973), p. 311.

20. Don N. Page, "Inflation Does Not Explain Time Asymmetry," *Nature*, vol. 304, July 7, 1983, p. 39.

21. Ibid., p. 40.

22. Miller, "The New Myth: A Critique of New Age Ideology," p. 26.

23. Henry M. Morris, *Acts & Facts*, (Institute of Creation Research), vol. 14, no. 11, November 1985, p. 1.

24. Henry M. Morris, *The Biblical Basis for Modern Science* (Grand Rapids: Baker, 1984), pp. 56, 57.

25. From a letter to Elliot Miller, dated April 11, 1986. Quoted in Miller, "The New Myth: A Critique of New Age Ideology," p. 27.

26. Hexham and Poewe-Hexham, "The Soul of the New Age," p. 21.

27. John Keel, *The Eighth Tower* (New York: Signet, 1975), p. 42. Quoted in Albrecht and Alexander, "The Sellout of Science," p. 20.

28. Henry M. Morris, *King of Creation* (San Diego: C.L.P. Publishers, 1980), p. 111.

29. From class notes, Fall semester, 1984, "Apologetic Systems," Dr. Walter R. Martin, professor, The Simon Greenleaf School of Law.

30. See Albert Einstein's *Special Theory of Relativity*, (1905), for his explanations of our elliptical universe. Specific statements concerning Einstein's unified field theory are further derived from class notes, Fall semester, 1984, Martin, ibid.

31. Jill Gerston, *The Tacoma News Tribune*, 1 November 1987, p. E–1.

32. Ibid.

33. Dean C. Halverson, "Lifespring and the Sovereignty of Subjectivism," *SCP Journal*, Winter 1981–82, p. 25.

34. *Graduate Review* (magazine of the organization), Nov. 1976, p. 3. Quoted by Stanley Dokupil and Brooks Alexander, "Est: The Philosophy of Self-Worship," *SCP Journal*, Winter 1981–82, p. 21.

35. Ibid., p. 4. Quoted by Dokupil and Alexander, ibid., p. 21.

36. *East-West Journal*, September 1974. Quoted by Dokupil and Alexander, ibid., p. 21.

37. Walter Martin, *The New Cults* (Santa Ana: Vision, 1980), p. 113.

38. George Orwell, *Nineteen Eighty-Four* (New York: The American Library, Signet Classics, 1961), p. 205. Quoted by Martin, The New Cults, p. 115.

39. Jerry Rubin, "The est things in Life Aren't Free," *Crawdaddy*, Feb. 1976. Quoted by Martin, *The New Cults*, p. 126.

40. *Graduate Review*, Nov. 1976, p. 10. Quoted by Weldon and Wilson, *Occult Shock and Psychic Forces*, p. 314.

41. Werner Erhard, "The Transformation of est," *Graduate Review*, Nov. 1976. Quoted by Martin, *The New Cults*, p. 136.

42. Geisler, *Christian Apologetics*, p. 189.

43. Weldon and Wilson, *Occult Shock and Psychic Forces*, p. 117.

44. Josh McDowell and Don Stewart, *Understanding the Occult* (San Bernardino: Here's Life Publishers, 1982), p. 28.

45. Michel Gauquelin, *The Cosmic Clocks* (Chicago: Henry Regnery Co., 1967), p. 78. Quoted in McDowell and Stewart, *Understanding the Occult*, p. 28.

46. Ibid.

47. Quoted in Weldon and Wilson, *Occult Shock and Psychic Forces*, p. 118.

48. David Spangler, *Reflections on the Christ* (Farres, Scotland: Lecture series, 1978), p. 44.

49. Alexander, "Occult Philosophy and Mystical Experience," p. 17.

50. Dick Sutphen, *Master of Life*, no. 40, September 1988, p. 8.

6 | The Resurrection of Jesus Christ and the New Age

The impoverished world view of the New Age myth is an unreliable source for the socio-political problems that face our world (chapter five). Belief in New Age ideology is therefore unreasonable.

Through a comparison of world views, the purpose of this chapter is to demonstrate the reasonableness of the Christian faith, contrary to the unreasonableness of the New Age. The Christian world view is: (1) capable of competently addressing the great issues of our present day and (2) substantiated by reliable primary-source documents (biblical revelation).

The Christian claim is that the Creator of the universe has appeared in history as a man, Jesus of Nazareth. Therefore, Christianity is founded upon the person of Jesus Christ in relationship to his life, death, and resurrection. Contrary to the New Age, which is an unverifiable, nonhistorical myth, Christianity is historical by nature and can therefore be intellectually defended as a means to establishing its truth-claims.

Historical events are theologically interpreted within the context of the Christian world view. The cornerstone of the Christian faith, as to its veracity, is the factualness of the Resurrection as an actual historical event.

The Bible (Christianity's primary-source documents) interprets the resurrection of Jesus Christ as the revelation of the living God, making known to all men "the God who is there" (Acts 17:23, 24). Further, God alone, according to the Old Testament (Deuteronomy 32:39; 1 Samuel 2:6), is able to give life to his creatures and through his power to raise them from the dead (Psalms 2:7). Absolutely no doubt was present in the minds of Jews contemporary with Jesus as to his claims to deity when he proclaimed: "For as the Father raiseth up the dead, and quickeneth them; even so the Son quickeneth whom he will" (John 5:21).

The Resurrection then is the supreme attestation of Jesus Christ's claims to deity (John 2:19–21; 8:58; 10:30; 11:25; 20:27, 28). If this "Grand Miracle" of the New Testament is a falsehood, Christians would be "of all men most miserable" (1 Corinthians 15:19), and Christianity would be nothing more than a pernicious myth itself, in league with the New Age. However, if true, the resurrection of Jesus Christ is the most incomparable event in human history. For all men would then ultimately be accountable to the sovereign holy God of the Bible, who alone is worthy of our worship, and who will judge all mankind by his Son, Jesus Christ, whom he has raised triumphantly from the grave as a promise of eternal life to everyone that would place their faith in him as their Lord and Savior (Acts 2:24; 4:12; Romans 2:16).

In speaking of death as the ultimate human malady, British barrister John Warwick Montgomery confronts us with the full weight of the Christian claim that Christ is indeed risen: "If Christ did in fact conquer this most basic of all human enemies and claimed on the basis of it to be God incarnate, able to give eternal life to those who believe in him, it would be sheer madness not to take with full seriousness the biblical affirmation that 'God was in Christ reconciling the world unto himself.' "[1]

In critiquing the Christian world view, specifically the resurrection of Jesus Christ, Simon Greenleaf, considered the greatest authority on common law evidence in the nineteenth century and a member of the Royall Professorship of Law at the Harvard Law School, insists that "All that Christianity asks of men on this subject, is, that they would be consistent with themselves; that they would treat its evidences as they treat the evidence of other things; and that they would try and judge its actors and witnesses, as they deal with their fellow men, when testifying to human affairs and actions, in human tribunals."[2]

A Legal-Historical Case for the Resurrection[3]

Former United States Supreme Court Justice Fuller stated: "The existing evidence of Christ's resurrection is satisfactory to me. I have not examined it from the legal standpoint, but Greenleaf has done so, and he is the highest authority on evidence cited in our courts."[4] Greenleaf's work, *Laws of Evidence*, was a standard textbook in English-speaking law schools throughout the world for several years.

Greenleaf established legal testimony upon five points: (1) honesty; (2) ability (competence of those testifying); (3) the number (referring to witnesses) and the consistency of the witnesses' testimony; (4) the conformity of the testimony to human experience; (5) the conformity of the witnesses' testimony with collateral circumstances (does adequate historical evidence exist and does it agree with historians contemporary to the testimony under scrutiny?).[5] We will examine the claims of the disciples of Jesus Christ in accord with these five legal points.

The Honesty of the Disciples

Unless a motive for lying can be established, men are usually presumed to be telling the truth. This is a universal presumption applied in courts of law, even when the integrity of the witness is questionable.[6]

In considering the testimony of Jesus' disciples of their Lord's resurrection, we must note that their claims were contrary to all of their worldly interests. They consistently preached that Christ had suffered a cruel death, followed by his resurrection from the dead, and that this established his claims as the Savior of the world. Although they faced extreme opposition that resulted in the martyrdom of all but one apostle and a great number of the other disciples, they continued to claim that God had demonstrated his willingness to redeem fallen man through the power of Christ's resurrection.

Every conceivable motive existed for the disciples to examine the basis for their faith through reflection upon the evidences for it. Greenleaf contends that "It was therefore impossible that they could have persisted in affirming the truths they have narrated, had not Jesus actually risen from the dead, and had they not known this fact as certainly as they knew any other fact."[7]

British legal authority J. N. D. Anderson agrees with Greenleaf that the apostles would have broken under pressure had Jesus not risen from the dead. To consider otherwise "would run totally contrary to all we know of the disciples: their ethical teaching, the quality of their lives, their steadfastness in suffering and persecution. Nor would it begin to explain their dramatic transformation from dejected and dispirited escapists into witnesses whom no opposition could muzzle."[8]

In his book, *Loving God*, Charles Colson, former Watergate conspirator, documents the events that led to the conviction of some of the most powerful men in the world after they failed to cover-up the infamous American political scandal that was exposed in the Spring of 1973.[9] Colson comments: "With the most powerful office in the world at stake, a small band of hand-picked loyalists, no more than ten of us, could not hold a conspiracy together for more than two weeks . . . after just a few weeks the natural human instinct for self-preservation was so overwhelming that the conspirators, one by one, deserted their leader, walked away from their cause, turned their backs on the power, prestige, and privileges."[10] In like manner, the terrified disciples fled from their betrayed Master on the eve of his hideous death by crucifixion (Matthew 26:56). And yet, what explanation, apart from having actually seen their Lord risen from the dead, can be given for the undaunted courage possessed by the disciples only days following their Lord's cruel execution?

A claim that the disciples were dishonest is so far-fetched that even opponents of Christianity such as D. F. Strauss admit: "The historian must acknowledge that the disciples firmly believed that Jesus was risen."[11] Jewish scholar Joseph Klausner also concedes the impeccable character of the disciples, noting that they were much too honorable to perpetrate a deception.[12]

Even if the disciples would not have deceived others, this does not mean that they themselves could not have been deceived. Among those who had access to the tomb of Christ were three groups who could have taken the body of Jesus of Nazareth: (1) the Romans; (2) the Jewish religious authorities; (3) the disciples. In consideration of both the Romans and the Jews, no possible motive can be established, for it would have been against their interests to have taken the body of Jesus. The Romans were concerned with collecting taxes and keeping peace in the Jewish state. Jesus of Nazareth had caused enough turmoil as far as Pontius Pilate was concerned. Therefore, a Roman theft of Christ's body would have only created more chaos within Israel and chanced the swift, unmerciful judgement of the Caesar in Rome.

As for the Jews, they were committed to refuting the claims of Jesus. All the Jewish religious leaders would have had to do was to produce the slain body of Jesus of Nazareth and Christianity would have immediately been exposed a fraud.

We have already provided testimony relating to the integrity of the disciples as far as deception is concerned; however, John W. Montgomery's observation serves us well in demonstrating that the disciples were not themselves deceivers: "It passes the bounds of credibility that the early Christians could have manufactured such a tale and then preached it among those who might easily have refuted it simply by producing the body of Jesus."[13]

Consider the possibility that the disciples were treacherous enough to fool their adversaries into believing that they were men of great character. Greenleaf argues that "it is impossible to read their writings, and not feel that we are conversing with men eminently holy, and of tender consciences, with men acting under an abiding sense of the presence and omniscience of God, and of their accountability to him, living in his fear, and walking in his ways."[14]

The disciples were committed to lives of personal sacrifice, humiliation, loneliness, revilement, and oftentimes lacking in sustenance. Why wouldn't bad men rather invent a religion that was more self-serving, which is compatible with human nature and characteristic of sinister cults, instead of spreading teachings that would deprive them of any worldly pleasures? It is incredible for us to think that bad men would "promote the religion of the God of truth."[15]

If the disciples believed in heaven and hell, they would have most assuredly reserved for themselves a place in the latter. If they did not believe in either heaven or hell, then why would they produce falsehoods that would only serve to make their lives miserable, destroying all hope of happiness in this world?[16]

Such legal reasoning, as applied to the resurrection, is inescapable, as is the evidence of the transformed lives of the disciples. These men did, in fact, testify "to that which they had carefully observed and considered and well knew to be true."[17]

The Competence of the Witnesses (Ability)

The competence of a witness depends on "the opportunities which he has had for observing the fact, the accuracy of his powers of discerning, and the faithfulness of his memory in retaining the facts, once observed and known."[18] We do not possess any historical evidence that would incriminate the disciples as far as their ability to comprehend and deal with facts. Unless the objector can provide evidence to the contrary, however, we are at liberty to assume that they were like the rest of their own contemporaries. Greenleaf notes that it is a uniform presumption of law (until proven otherwise) that men are honest, of sound mind, and ordinary intelligence.[19] As a tax collector, Matthew was professionally trained to be very suspicious in his dealing with people and facts. Luke, as well, was acutely trained in his powers of observation as a physician. As far as the other two Gospel writers are concerned, they simply were much too unlearned to construct such a clever forgery that would escape detection by their critics.

Number and Consistency

More than 500 eyewitnesses saw the risen Christ following his passion on Calvary in at least seventeen post–resurrection appearances. In his first letter to the Corinthians (chapter 15), the Apostle Paul challenged the Corinthians to go and ask any of several hundred eyewitnesses, who were themselves still alive and available to testify to the risen Savior.

There exist enough differences among the writers of the New Testament so as to discount any allegations of conspiracy. Yet, at the same time, such substantial agreement exists among the inspired authors so as to demonstrate that they in fact were all well acquainted with the same great historical event.

Greenleaf argues that "The discrepancies between the narratives of the several evangelists, when carefully examined, will not be found sufficient to invalidate their testimony. Many seeming contradictions will prove, upon closer scrutiny, to be in substantial agreement; and it may be confidently asserted that there are none that will not yield, under fair and just criticism."[20]

It must be further noted, that if the different Gospel accounts were all the same, then the skeptic would have a good case for collusion. The author's accounts rather provide us with a built-in means to cross-examine each of them. This is non-existent outside of the Christian faith.

The Conformity of the Disciples' Testimony with Human Experience

This legal test of the validity of Christian claims raises the issue of miracles. The objector contends that miracles are impossible. Therefore, the New Testament narratives are superstitious accounts of foolish individuals that are unworthy of the world's belief. Science is often appealed to as a disclaimer of Christian claims to the miraculous.

Since historical Christianity is inseparable from its claims to the miraculous, this category of legal examination is crucial to the Christian claim that Jesus Christ has conquered death through his resurrection.

Without Christian theism, modern science would not have been possible. Sir Francis Bacon, a devout believer in the Bible and Lord Chancellor of England, founded and established the "scientific method" in science, not by relying upon the philosophical deduction of Aristotle, but with reference to the reality of the created order of the systems of the universe.

Consider further some of the great scientific discoveries and developments in science by men, who as Christians, interpreted their observations in accord with a Christian world view: Isaac Newton (dynamics), Johann Kepler (astronomy), Robert Boyle (chemistry), Lord Kelvin (thermodynamics), Louis Pasteur (bacteriology), Matthew Maury, (oceanography), Michael Faraday (electromagnetics), Clerk Maxwell (electrodynamics), John Ray (biology), and Carolus Linnaeus (taxonomy).[21]

These scientific discoveries and developments were possible because of three basic axioms of science: "The first of the unprovable premises on which science has been based is the belief that the world is real and the human mind is capable of knowing its real nature. . . . The second and best known postulate underlying the structure of scientific knowledge is that of cause and effect. . . . The third basic scientific premise is that nature is unified."[22] These three axioms are basically Christian in origin and nature, concludes scientist Stanley D. Beck.[23]

The major divisions of science reflect the creation of the universe by the personal God of the Bible. The biblical commandment of God to man to take "dominion" over the earth (Genesis 1:28) must be understood in its proper context. Henry Morris points out that,

> There are only three specific acts of "ex nihilo" creation recorded in Genesis, indicating three fundamentally different entities in God's universe. These acts are indicated by the use of the verb "create" (Hebrew *bara'*):
>
> 1. In the beginning God "created" the heaven and the earth (Genesis 1:1).
>
> 2. God "created" . . . every living creature that moveth (Genesis 2:21).
>
> 3. God "created" man in his own image (Genesis 1:27).[24]

Genesis 1:1 refers to the creation of the world. Genesis 2:21 relates to all living creatures except God's special creation in his own image as recorded in Genesis 1:27. These three major categories of God's creation provide a basis for the physical sciences, the life sciences, and the sociohumanistic sciences (inclusive of the social-behavioral sciences and humanities).[25]

The concept of the "dominion" mandate of Genesis is the basis for many of the great scientific discoveries that benefit the Western world. Medical advancements, hospitals, the American Red Cross, and scores of international relief agencies and efforts are based upon the Christian ethic and world view. The great institutions of education (e.g., Harvard, Yale, Princeton) in this nation and in Europe owe their origins to Christianity. To be sure, the New Age world view (not to mention atheistic humanism, existentialism, and other world views) is little more than a parasite on the Judeo-Christian world view.

Dr. Abraham Wolf, former professor and head of the Department of the History and Method of Science at the University of London, defines the scientific concept of cause and effect:

> Except among believers in magic, at the one extreme, and among thoroughgoing skeptics, at the other extreme, it is usually assumed either explicitly or at least implicitly, that every event has a cause, and that the same kind of cause has the same kind of effect. This assumption is commonly known as the Postulate or Principle of Universal Causation.[26]

The new science rejects this definition and claims that its origin is purely prescribed by the "anthropomorphic" God of Christianity. However, Wolf brilliantly points out the fallacy of such reasoning:

> The principle of conservation of matter or energy would lose all significance without the idea of causal continuity, according to which certain successive events not only "follow," but "follow from," one another. In fact, mere laws of sequence are only intelligible in the resort, when they can be shown to result from direct or indirect causal connections.[27]

The Principle of Universal Causation assumes the two laws of thermodynamics, which govern all natural processes. Henry M. Morris demonstrates the viability of the Christian world view in relationship to scientific realities:

> The first law of thermodynamics, states (in accordance with Genesis 2:1–3) that none of the tremendous energy (or "power") of the universe is now being created, so that the universe could not have created itself. The second law (in accordance with Romans 8:20–22, as well as Genesis 3:17–19) states that the available energy of the universe is decreasing, indicating

that sometime in the past all the energy (including matter) was available and perfectly organized, like a clock that had just been wound up. This shows that the universe must have been created, even though it could not create itself. The two laws thus point inexorably back to Genesis 1:1."[28]

Obviously the source of the universe is beyond the finite dimensions of space and time. The power that both created and sustains the universe must be eternal, and therefore, omnipotent. Instead of manufacturing an imaginary law such as "syntropy," the Christian world view stands firmly upon the revelation of the omnipotent Creator and sustainer of the universe (Genesis 1:1; John 1:3; Colossians 1:17).

The first and second law of thermodynamics further demonstrate that the pantheistic world view of the New Age could not possibly explain the existence of the universe or become a basis for scientific inquiry. The nature of the universe rather points to an infinite first cause, such as revealed in the Bible. Having examined the compatability of Christian faith and scientific method in general, let us examine the more specific issue of miracles.

David Hume, an eighteenth-century skeptic philosopher, was one of the most formidable opponents to the possibility of miracles. Hume based his argument on the nature of natural law. In speaking of Hume, Greenleaf notes, "He deduces the existence of such immutable laws from the uniform course of human experience. This, he affirms, is our only guide in reasoning concerning matters of fact; and whatever is contrary to human experience, he pronounces incredible."[29]

Hume stressed that the laws of nature are based on the highest degree of probability. Norman Geisler summarizes Hume's argument against the possibility of miracles as follows:

(1) A miracle by definition is a violation of (or exception to) a law of nature;

(2) But the laws of nature are built upon the highest degree of probability;

(3) Hence, a miracle by definition (as an exception) is based on the lowest degree of probability;

(4) Now the wise man should always base his belief on the highest degree of probability;

(5) Therefore, the wise man should never believe in miracles.[30]

Hume's argument is based upon a fallacious definition of the term miracle. Rather than a "violation" of natural laws, biblical miracles are unique events, taking place within history, having an evidential value and requiring a religious explanation. It must be further stressed that a biblical miracle is not an "unnatural" event, but a supernatural event.

Miracles are a priori impossible in Hume's naturalistic thinking. Hume presupposes the impossibility of miracles and then "proves" that they are impossible. As to the fourth premise of Hume's argument, why should the wise man always believe in the highest degree of probability as based on past experience? Geisler observes that "Even Hume argued that we cannot be sure the sun will rise tomorrow simply because it has always risen in the past. There is no necessary connection between the past and the present, as Hume would be the first to admit."[31]

Concerning the error of Hume, Greenleaf asserts that "Without stopping to examine the correctness of this doctrine, as a fundamental principle in the law of evidence, it is sufficient in this place to remark, that it contains this fallacy; it excludes all knowledge derived by inference or deduction from facts, confining us to what we derive from experience alone, and thus depriving us of any knowledge, or even rational belief, of the existence or character of God."[32]

Rather than living in a programmed universe (a universe where natural laws are immutable) we live in a contingent, open (unprogrammed) universe (as demonstrated inductively in chapter five). C. S. Lewis observes:

> The dazzlingly obvious conclusion now arose in my mind: in the whole history of the universe laws of nature have never produced a single event. They are the pattern to which every event must conform, provided only that it can be induced to happen. But how do you get it to do that? How do you get a move on: The laws of nature can give you no help there. All events obey them, just as all operations with money obey the laws of arithmetic. . . . Up till now I had had a vague idea that the laws of nature could make things happen. I now saw that this was exactly like thinking that you could increase your income by doing sums about it. The laws are the pattern to which events conform: the source of events must be sought elsewhere.[33]

Henry Morris, in support of Lewis's observation, concludes that, "The occurrence of a miracle does not contravene causality but merely invokes a higher cause, a cause quite adequate to produce the miracle."[34] The principle of causation testifies to a personal, omnipotent God with regard to the issue of miracles.

Furthermore, a truly biblical miracle requires a moral-theological explanation. A biblical miracle points to its source (the living God), whereas an occult phenomenon is nonevidential and amoral, pointing to the individual performing an alleged supernatural act.

John Warwick Montgomery concludes our argument concerning the possibility of miracles, including the "grand miracle" of the Christian faith as follows:

> To oppose the resurrection on the ground that miracles do not occur is, as we have noted earlier, both philosophically and scientifically irresponsible: philosophically, because no one below the status of a god could know the universe so well as to eliminate miracles a priori; and scientifically, because in the age of Einsteinian physics, . . . the universe has opened up to all possibilities, . . . and only a careful consideration of the empirical testimony for a miraculous event can determine whether in fact it has or has not occurred.[35]

In the final analysis, "Only the primary-source evidence for an event can ultimately determine whether it occurred or not, and only that same evidence will establish the proper interpretation of the event."[36]

In the case of the New Testament, miracles are factually presented, in plain, intelligible terms and as having publicly taken place. The messianic credentials of Jesus of Nazareth are attested to by eyewitnesses of his power to heal: "The blind receive their sight, and the lame walk, the lepers are cleansed and the deaf hear, the dead are raised" (Matthew 11:5). With reference to the miracles of the New Testament, Simon Greenleaf concludes: "If they were separately testified to, by different witnesses of ordinary intelligence and integrity, in any court of justice, the jury would be bound to believe them."[37]

The Conformity of the Witnesses' Testimony with Collateral Circumstances

Simon Greenleaf contends that "it is not possible for the wit of man to invent a story, which, if closely compared with the actual occurrences of the same time and place, may not be shown to be false."[38] A false witness is very hesitant to provide details that could possibly lead to the exposure of inconsistencies in his testimony. False witnesses, therefore, speak in broad generalizations, whereas true witnesses willingly provide details without any apparent concern of the detection of inconsistencies in their testimony.[39]

Can we test the reliability of the testimony of the disciples in the New Testament narratives? We must submit the New Testament documents to the same tests as any other narratives from antiquity in order to answer this question. This test is foundational to the preceding four tests, and when established through a legal-historical method, it removes the claims of this apologetic from accusations of circular reasoning.

Military historian, Professor C. Sanders, sets forth three tests necessary to determine the trustworthiness of ancient documents: the bibliographical, internal, and external tests.[40]

Bibliographical Test

Montgomery explains the purpose of this test:

This first test refers to the analysis of the textual tradition by which a document reaches us. In the case of the New Testament documents, the question is this: Not having the original copies, can we reconstruct them well enough to see what they say Jesus claimed?[41]

Sir Frederic G. Kenyon, formerly the director and principal librarian of the British Museum, demonstrates the superiority of the New Testament over other ancient manuscripts with regard to the bibliographical test: "In no other case is the interval of time between the composition of the book and the date of the earliest extant manuscripts so short as in that of the New Testament. The books of the New Testament were written in the latter part of the first century; the earliest extant manuscripts (trifling scraps excepted) are of the fourth century—say, from 250 to 300 years later. This may sound a considerable interval, but it is nothing to that which parts most of the great classical authors from their earliest manuscripts. We believe that we have in all essentials an accurate text of the seven extant plays of Sophocles; yet the earliest substantial manuscript upon which it is based was written more than 1400 years after the poet's death. Aeschylus, Aristophanes, and Thucydides are in the same state; while with Euripides the interval is increased to 1600 years. For Plato it may be put at 1300 years, for Demosthenes as low as 1200."[42]

Following Kenyon's original bibliographical attestation to the New Testament, several papyri were discovered that dated back to the end of the first century, bringing the time interval between the actual composition of the primary source documents and the copies to within but a few years.[43] These discoveries prompted Kenyon to write: "The interval, then, between the dates of original composition and the earliest extant evidence becomes so small as to be in fact negligible, and the last foundation for any doubt that the Scriptures have come down to us substantially as they were written has now been removed. Both the authenticity and the general integrity of the books of the New Testament may be regarded as finally established."[44]

Greek New Testament scholar A. T. Robertson has further substantiated the New Testament bibliographically, commenting that "There are some 8,000 manuscripts of the Latin Vulgate and at least 1,000 for the other early versions. Add over 4,000 Greek manuscripts and we have 13,000 manuscript copies of portions of the New Testament. Besides all this, much of the New Testament can be reproduced from the quotations of the early Christian writers."[45] Princeton University's Bruce Metzger accounts for a total of 4,969 New Testament Greek manuscripts.[46]

This conclusion compels John Montgomery to write: "To be skeptical of the resultant text of the New Testament books is to allow all of classical antiquity to slip into obscurity, for no documents of the ancient period are as well attested bibliographically as the New Testament."[47]

Internal Test

In this second test, historical and literary scholarship continues to follow Aristotle's dictum that the benefit of the doubt is to be given to the document itself, not arrogated by the critic to himself. This means that one must listen to the claims of the document under analysis and not assume fraud or error unless the author disqualifies himself by contradictions or known factual inaccuracies.[48]

The first disciples of Jesus Christ claimed to be eyewitnesses of his life, death, and resurrection: "And he that saw it bare record, and his record is true: and he knoweth that he saith true, that ye might believe" (John 19:35; Also: Luke 1:1–4; Acts 2:32; I John 1:1–3; etc.). The value of this claim is inestimable when considering the truthfulness of the resurrection within a legal context.

F. F. Bruce, Professor Emeritus at the University of Manchester, astutely observes that:

> It was not only friendly eyewitnesses that the early preachers had to reckon with; there were others less well disposed who were also conversant with

the main facts of the ministry and death of Jesus. The disciples could not afford to risk inaccuracies (not to speak of willful manipulation of the facts), which would at once be exposed by those who would be only too glad to do so. On the contrary, one of the strong points in the original apostolic preaching is the confident appeal to the knowledge of the hearers; they not only said "we are witnesses of these things," but also "As you yourselves also know" (Acts 2:22). Had there been any tendency to depart from the facts in any material respect, any hostile witnesses in the audience would have served as a further corrective.[49]

Hostile witnesses within the vicinity of Jerusalem would have been extremely anxious to expose the gospel message as a hoax. William F. Albright, formerly of Johns Hopkins University and a renowned biblical archaeologist, supported the internal claims of the New Testament as an eyewitness account: "In my opinion, every book of the New Testament was written by a baptized Jew between the forties and the eighties of the first century A.D. (Very probably sometime between about A.D. 50 and 75)."[50]

External Test

The external test asks the question: "Do other historical materials confirm or deny the internal testimony provided by the documents themselves?"[51]

External testimony from contemporary writers consistently confirms the claims of the New Testament. The following examples will establish this point as fact.

The Roman historian, Cornelius Tacitus (A.D. 112) writes of the death of Jesus Christ and the present influence of Christians in Rome. Tacitus states that Jesus was put to death by Pontius Pilate during the reign of Tiberius (*Annals* XV. 44). Tacitus further mentions the burning of the temple in Jerusalem in A.D. 70 and mentions Christianity within that context (*Histories*, Chron. ii.30.6).

Lucian of Samosata, a second-century satirist, ridiculed Christianity. Lucian spoke of the rejection of polytheism by Christians and stated that the primitive Christian Church worshipped Jesus like a god. He also refers to the crucifixion of Jesus Christ in Palestine (*The Passing of Peregrinus*).

A contemporary of Christ's, Jewish historian Josephus (A.D. 37–100), documents numerous familiar figures mentioned in the New Testament. As observed by F. F. Bruce:

Here, in the pages of Josephus, we meet many figures who are well known to us from the New Testament: the colourful family of the Herods; the Roman emperors Augustus, Tiberius, Claudius, and Nero; Quirinius, the governor of Syria; Pilate, Felix, and Festus, the procurators of Judea; the high priestly families—Annas, Caiaphas, Ananias, and the rest; the Pharisees and the Sadducees; and so on.[52]

Another Roman historian, Suetonius (c. A.D. 120) refers to the persecution of Christians by Nero (*Life of the Caesars*, 26.2). In a letter, dated A.D. 73, a Syrian named Mara Bar-Serapian mentions the death of Jesus Christ in addition to the deaths of Socrates and Pythagoras. This letter is presently preserved at the British Museum.[53]

Pliny the Younger (c. A.D. 112) noted in a letter that Christians worshipped Jesus Christ as a god and that they came together once a week to sing hymns to their Savior. He mentions his own persecution of Christians and his having killed many of them while governor of Bithynia. He stated that he tried to force Christians to "curse Christ, which a genuine Christian cannot be induced to do" (*Epistles* X.96).

The Jewish Talmud, in referring to the ministry of Jesus of Nazareth, attributes his miracles to a satanic origin, further stating that he was born of an adulteress and that he was crucified on the eve of the Passover (*Sanhedrin* 43a, "Eve of Passover;" and *Yebamoth* 4, 3; 49a). The New Testament details even these accusations as they fell from the lips of the Pharisees (Mark 3:22; John 8:41).

It is most noteworthy that external, non-Christian references substantiate the internal claims of the Christian Gospel as to its most central points: (1) Jesus was worshipped and believed to be deity; (2) Jesus performed miracles; (3) Jesus was crucified under Pontius Pilate, in Palestine, during the Passover; (4) the earth was darkened on the day of his crucifixion; (5) the primitive Church rejected polytheism; (6) Nero, among other Roman rulers, persecuted the Christian Church; (7) the Jews accused Jesus of being illegitimate, affirming at least that Joseph was not his real father, and further attributed his miracles to Satan; and finally that (8) The ministry of Jesus of Nazareth was during the reign of Tiberius Caesar.[54]

William F. Albright further confirms the trustworthiness of the New Testament documents by citing the wealth of archaeological evidence in support of their reliability: "The excessive skepticism shown toward the Bible by important historical schools of the eighteenth and nineteenth centuries, certain phases of which still appear periodically, has been progressively discredited. Discovery after discovery has established the accuracy of innumerable details, and has brought increased recognition to the value of the Bible as a source of history."[55]

Conclusion

The evidence for the resurrection of Jesus Christ, as based on eyewitness testimony and established under legal cross-examination, is so substantial that any jury, in any court of law, would be compelled to accept it as an actual historical event. Greenleaf concludes: "Either the men of Galilee were men of superlative wisdom, and extensive knowledge and experience, and of deeper skill in the arts of deception than any and all others, before or after them, or they have truly stated the astonishing things which they saw and heard."[56]

The Judeo-Christian world view is able to bring mankind into a threefold relationship: (1) proper relationship with the world around us, offering hope and resolution for the problems facing us in this present day of crisis; (2) proper relationship to one another as a basis for human rights, for the Judeo-Christian world view establishes the self-worth of an individual upon his special creation in the image of God; and (3) proper relationship with the living God through faith in the risen Lord and Savior Jesus Christ (Romans 10:9, 10).

The Apostle Peter states: "For we have not followed cunningly devised fables, when we made known unto you the power and coming of our Lord Jesus Christ, but were eyewitnesses of his majesty" (II Peter 1:16). The word rendered "fables" is the Greek word *mythos*, from which we get the word myths. The Christian faith is not founded upon empty, unsubstantiated myths, such as the New Age, but rather it is founded upon the incontrovertible self-disclosure of the living God to mankind as revealed in history and embodied in Jesus Christ (Colossians 2:9).

The Christian faith is reasonable, and the denial of Christianity is unreasonable. This does not reduce faith to reason, but rather provides a substantiated foundation for the Christian faith; the historical event of Christ's resurrection from the dead. The Christian does not trust in a metaphor, but in a real, risen Savior in approaching God by faith (Hebrews 11:6).

In an ancient city near Kapilvastu, India, archaeologists uncovered a large sandstone casket. The inscription on the casket indicated that the mortal remains of Gautama Buddha were contained within it.

Instead of choosing between "Buddha or the Bomb," the risen Savior and Lord Jesus Christ offers a more sure way.

The Christian faith looks forward to "the blessed hope" of the earthly return of the Lord Jesus Christ who will bring in a glorious new age. Instead of sinful man, the thorn-crowned King of kings and Lord of lords, Jesus Christ, will reign in the blessed new age to come (Revelation 22:1–7).

Notes to Chapter 6

1. John Warwick Montgomery, ed., *Christianity for the Toughminded* (Minneapolis: Bethany House, 1973), p. 32.

2. Simon Greenleaf, *The Testimony of the Evangelists* (Grand Rapids: Baker, 1984), p. 46.

3. Unless otherwise quoted, the legal reasoning contained within this chapter is a paraphrase of the reasoning of Greenleaf, *The Testimony of the Evangelists*.

4. Simon Greenleaf, "Why I Believe," *Book Fellowship*, North Syracuse, N.Y., p. 7.

5. Greenleaf, *The Testimony of the Evangelists*, p. 28.

6. Ibid., pp. 31, 32.

7. Greenleaf, *The Testimony of the Evangelists*, p. 29.

8. J. N. D. Anderson, *Christianity: The Witness of History* (Downers Grove: InterVarsity Press, 1970), p. 92.

9. The Watergate scandal refers to the breaking into and bugging of the Democratic National Committee offices by a group of ex-Cuban freedom fighters who were enlisted by key individuals within the Republican administration during the presidency of Richard M. Nixon.

10. Charles Colson, *Loving God* (Grand Rapids: Zondervan, 1983), p. 67.

11. D. F. Strauss, *Das Leben Jesu* (Darmstadt: Wissenschaftliche Buchgesellschaft, 1835), p. 289.

12. Joseph Klausner, *Jesus of Nazareth* (New York: Macmillan, 1925), p. 414.

13. Josh McDowell, *The Resurrection Factor* (San Bernardino: Here's Life Publishers, 1981), p. 89.

14. Greenleaf, *The Testimony of the Evangelists*, p. 30.

15. Ibid., p. 31.

16. Ibid.

17. Ibid.

18. Ibid.

19. Ibid.

20. Ibid., p. 33. Also see Gleason Archer, *An Encyclopedia of Bible Difficulties* (Minneapolis: Bethany House, 1982), for a scholarly and exhaustive treatment of alleged contradictions in the Bible.

21. Morris, *The Biblical Basis for Modern Science*, p. 30. For an exhaustive list of Christians and their contributions to science, see Henry M. Morris, *Men of Science, Men of God*, (San Diego: Master Book Publishers, 1984).

22. Stanley D. Beck, "Natural Science and Creationist Theology," *Bioscience* 32 (Oct. 1982), p. 739. Quoted in Morris, *The Biblical Basis for Modern Science*, pp. 30, 31.

23. Ibid., p. 31.

24. Ibid., p. 42.

25. Ibid.

26. *Encyclopedia Britannica*, 1949 ed., s.v. "Causality, or Causation," by Abraham Wolf. Quoted in Morris, *The Biblical Basis for Modern Science*, p. 35.

27. Ibid., p. 62. Quoted in Morris, *The Biblical Basis for Modern Science*, p. 35.

28. Ibid., p. 53.

29. Greenleaf, *The Testimony of the Evangelists*, p. 36.

30. Norman Geisler, *Christian Apologetics* (Grand Rapids: Baker, 1976), p. 266.

31. Ibid., pp. 266, 267. David Hume's admission is contained in his: *Enquiry Concerning Human Understanding*.

32. Greenleaf, *The Testimony of the Evangelists*, pp. 37, 38.

33. C. S. Lewis, *God in the Dock* (Grand Rapids: Eerdmans, 1970), p. 78.

34. Morris, *The Biblical Basis for Modern Science*, p. 36.

35. Montgomery, ed., *Christianity for the Toughminded*, pp. 31, 32.

36. John Warwick Montgomery, *Faith Founded on Fact* (Nashville: Thomas Nelson Publishers, 1978), p. 57.

37. Greenleaf, *The Testimony of the Evangelists*, p. 42.

38. Ibid., p. 45.

39. Ibid., pp. 43, 44.

40. C. Sanders, *Introduction to Research in English Literary History* (New York: Macmillan, 1952), pp. 143ff.

41. John Warwick Montgomery, *History and Christianity* (Minneapolis: Bethany House, 1965), p. 26.

42. Sir Frederic G. Kenyon, *Handbook to the Textual Criticism of the New Testament*, 2nd ed. (London: Macmillan, 1912), p. 5. Quoted in Montgomery, *History and Christianity*, p. 27.

43. See: F. W. Hall, "MS Authorities for the Text of the Chief Classical Writers," *Companion to Classical Texts* (Oxford: Clarendon Press, 1913), pp. 199ff., for a detailed chart comparing numerous other ancient texts with the New Testament bibliographically.

44. Sir Frederic G. Kenyon, *The Bible and Archaeology* (New York: Harper, 1940), pp. 288, 289.

45. A. T. Robertson, *Introduction to the Textual Criticism of the New Testament* (Nashville: Broadman Press, 1925), p. 70.

46. Bruce Metzger, *The Text of the New Testament* (New York: Oxford University Press, 1964), pp. 31–33.

47. Montgomery, *History and Christianity*, p. 29.

48. Ibid., p. 29.

49. F. F. Bruce, *The New Testament Documents: Are They Reliable?* (Grand Rapids: Eerdmans, 1960), p. 46.

50. William F. Albright (Interview), *Christianity Today*, January 18, 1963, p. 18.

51. Montgomery, *History and Christianity*, p. 31.

52. Bruce, *The New Testament Documents: Are They Reliable?* p. 104.

53. Ibid., p. 14.

54. These summary conclusions were drawn by: Francis Beckwith, *Baha'i* (Minneapolis: Bethany House, 1985), p. 50.

55. Albright, Interview, *Christianity Today*, p. 18. See also Donald J. Wiseman, "Archaeological Confirmation of the Old Testament," in Carl F. Henry, *Revelation and the Bible* (Waco: Word, 1979), pp. 301–2, who notes that over 25,000 archaeological discoveries have been made in the Holy Land. See also R. K. Harrison, *Introduction to the Old Testament* (Grand Rapids: Eerdmans, 1969). Harrison observes that he has "yet to become acquainted with any single archaeological find which by itself or in conjunction with others specifically and categorically disproves the testimony of the Old Testament" (p. 94).

56. Greenleaf, *The Testimony of the Evangelists*, p. 53.

7 | *Is It a Conspiracy?*

Is there a mysterious *They*—a conspiracy of powerful individuals plotting to take control of the world? Are *They* carrying out their devious plot through the manipulation of national economics, influencing foreign policy, assassinating heads of state, creating conditions of war, and maligning religious leaders?

The elusive *They* are shrouded with mystery and intrigue as they work behind the scenes of everyday life. *They* are veiled with obscurity as far as the unsuspecting public is concerned, but conspiracy theorists have taken up the challenge of snapping all of the puzzle parts together and identifying these sinister culprits as:

> communism, the illuminati, Neo-Nazism, the Mafia, the Rothschilds, international bankers, the Masons, the Catholic Church . . . the Council on foreign relations, the Rockefellers, the Tri-Lateral Commission, occultism, Zionism, the Bildebergers, satanism, etc. Some take the position that all of these are interconnected, highly organized and controlled by one mastermind, a political genius.[1]

Conspiracy theories have been the pursuit of many throughout human history. Many reflect a high degree of ingenuity and insight. Historically, conspiracy theories have been as diverse as they have been numerous. However, in spite of their diversity, the scenarios are unified by the common theme of "world conspiracy for world government."

Some conspiracy theorists are competent, qualified scholars; however, all too often they are also extremists guilty of oversimplifications and broad unfounded generalizations. Far-fetched allegations are so common that the serious scholar of a conspiracy theory is greatly handicapped in his efforts to establish a believable case. Competent conspiracy investigation usually deals with isolated historical events whereas the less competent world conspiracy theorists virtually ascribe sovereignty to *Them*.

History is seen merely as the machinations of the conspirators by many conspiracy theorists. Men are a part of a predetermined plan that meshes together like the gears of a machine. *They* are at the controls, directing all events in human history toward the fulfillment of their "New World Order." To fight against these evil designs, conspiracy theorists often build labyrinthine, teetering theories that are parodies of reason.

The New Age Conspiracy

The political agenda of the New Age (chapter three) has attracted numerous conspiracy theorists.[2] The basic plot is set forth, a conscious comprehensive conspiracy of individuals and organizations in league with the Devil to enthrone the Antichrist.

The Hidden Dangers of the Rainbow (Huntington House, 1983) by Constance Cumbey is the most influential book of this type to date. Mrs. Cumbey must be commended for her sincerity and zeal in exposing this nefarious world view. The New Age Movement is unquestionably hostile to historic Christianity. However, Mrs. Cumbey appears to be obsessed with her conspiratorial plot of the New Age to take over the world. According to Cumbey, the blueprint for world dominion by the New Age Movement was detailed in the late Alice Bailey's "plan:"

> One familiar with the Movement and the Bailey teachings cannot help but note the close patterning of developments within the New Age Movement along the lines set forth by Mrs. Bailey. She is literally followed like a recipe.[3]

The conspirators of the New Age, according to Cumbey, consciously follow an intricately detailed plan, cleverly designed to manipulate unrelated and spontaneous world events. The crowning event of the New Age coup would be the enthronement of "Maitreya" (Antichrist).

Benjamin Creme is an "artist and esotericist" who has studied and participated in the occult for over 20 years.[4] Creme grabs the spotlight in Mrs. Cumbey's book because he is a self-proclaimed spokesman for the coming "Christ" (Maitreya).

Benjamin Creme's announcement of "Maitreya the Christ" is the cul-
mination of over 100 years of meticulous planning and labor by those
seeking this "Age of Aquarius."[5]

A Faulty Scenario

Numerous problems exist with Mrs. Cumbey's conspiracy theory.
Principally, occult sources seem to inform her conclusions.

> For instance, her scenario depends heavily on two spiritually question-
> able sources which claim to describe the conspiracy: Alice Bailey (occult)
> and Marilyn Ferguson (New Age). While these two may be taken "seri-
> ously," they need not be taken "literally." Cumbey opens the door to
> distortion because she ignores the way occult and New Age propagan-
> dists weave conspiracy legends about themselves. She accepts their inflated
> self images at face value, but absorbs some of the unsavory spiritual im-
> plications as well: If Alice Bailey's "plan" is truly the blueprint for our
> future, it amounts to saying that demonic revelation can flesh out our
> understanding of divine revelation. It is giving the devil more than his
> due.[6]

The reduction of biblical revelation, cited by Alexander, affects
Cumbey's book to grave extremes. While it is true that conflict between
good and evil does take place within the human sphere (Ephesians 6:10–
18), this is, nonetheless, very limited in its dualistic context. Eschatological good and evil (ultimate good and evil) cannot, however, be reduced to the level of human scheming and manipulation. It is a denial
of the sovereignty of God to presume that all things are not under His
predetermined, providential control. God, apart from conscious, human
manipulation, will reveal the Antichrist (II Thess. 2:6–10). Men will
be used, beyond their full comprehension and conclusive understanding,
toward the fulfillment of evil ends (II Thess. 2:11–12), but they are no
more capable of enthroning the Antichrist through conscious effort than
the Church is able to bring Jesus Christ back to earth before His di-
vinely appointed time.

> When conspiracies mix with apocalypse, both act unfavorably on each
> other. The association sensationalizes the conspiracy and trivializes the
> apocalypse.[7]

The New Age Movement is better understood as the result of
a dynamic historical, cultural process (chapter two), rather than a conscious, monolithic conspiracy of international proportions and decades
of planning.

New Agers look to evolution as the explanation for their emerging world view. And yet, there is no doubt that Satan is injecting his venomous lies into the minds of men in an effort to lead them to ultimate destruction. However, rather than Alice Bailey's "plan," biblical revelation is a more reliable source of spiritual discernment.

There is no evidence of an overarching hierarchical structure controlling a unified New Age Movement. Many of the cults that subscribe to this world view (i.e., Eckankar, Church Universal and Triumphant, Divine Light Mission, est, Scientology, Lifespring, Silva Mind Control, Transcendental Meditation, etc.) are characterized by exclusivism and totalitarianism, as are all cults. Therefore, their respective leaders would not seek to share their throne of power with another.

The beliefs and emphases among many New Age groups can be quite diverse, and yet a common philosophical base can indicate a general consensus. In this limited sense, the New Age may be described as a conspiracy. However, this is true in the case of any world view to which people subscribe. To insist, therefore, that whenever one New Age leader speaks he/she speaks for the entire movement is very irresponsible reasoning.

Self-government growing out of self-deification is the ideal of the New Age. Among the majority of New Age advocates, the planetary paradise they envision emphasizes a political decentralization. A minority does seek a united order under one supreme ruler. The constituents of the minority primarily comprise those directly influenced by the Theosophical writings of Alice Bailey, as previously mentioned in chapter three.

Networking within the New Age Movement may impress some that a collusion committed to global totalitarianism exists. This would appear as an obvious evil, whereas a movement committed to global decentralization would not. Because the basic assumptions upon which the New Age edifice is founded are not obtrusive, the role of Networking within the movement can be misleading, provoking oversimplifications by those attempting to critique it. Movements organized along stringent lines (cults) are more easily identified and exposed; movements that are loosely knit structures (providing for more diversity of thought and experience) are not.

This observation in no sense diminishes the social-spiritual danger inherent in the New Age. On the contrary, the malignant spirituality and thinking of the New Age is allowed to creep into the minds of men like a tasteless, odorless gas under the defrauding guise of optimism. The intoxicating danger of the New Age is often difficult to discern.

> Unlike traditional Eastern mysticism, which tends to be reclusive, the New Age Movement is increasingly marked by efforts to penetrate society. The force behind this is an evolving ethic that stresses a balance between internal (personal) and external (social) transformation. New Agers would like to see as many people as possible experience "personal transformation," a psychic counterpart to a Christian new birth. But while Christianity openly demands a faith commitment, a conversion to New Age thinking can be provoked more subtly.[8]

It is apparent from Scripture that the perversion of the Gospel and the turning away of men from the Cross of Jesus Christ is the aim of the occult (Acts 13:8–10). This confronts the Christian Church with a great challenge to "contend earnestly for the faith once delivered" in presenting its message of the Cross.

A Biblical Perspective

The issue of conspiracy is not alien to the Old Testament. Adam and Eve conspired to escape the penetrating gaze of God following their act of disobedience (Gen. 3:8). Abraham and Sarah agreed to deceive King Abimelech to avoid persecution (Gen. 20:2), Jacob, with his mother's aid, tricked his father Isaac into believing he was Esau (Gen. 27:6–34), and Joseph was the victim of a diabolical plan by his brothers to do away with him (Gen 37:23–28). Balaam the prophet conspired with a Moabite king to curse Israel (Num. 22:15–31) and King David, in an attempt to cover up his sin with Bathsheba, orchestrated an elaborate scheme to kill Uriah (II Sam. 11:14–17). Absalom sought the throne of his father David through premeditated treachery (II Sam. 15:1–6); and in the book of Esther, Haman took advantage of his office in an attempt to exterminate the Jews (Esther 3).

The New Testament as well is acquainted with conspiratorial plots. The Sanhedrin were driven in their wickedness to destroy Jesus (Matt. 26:3, 4). Judas Iscariot aided and abetted the Sanhedrin, handing Jesus over to them for the agreed thirty pieces of silver (Matt. 26:47–50). The Judaizers, who were themselves "false brethren," sought to undermine the ministry of the Apostle Paul (Gal. 2:4).

Yet, the hand of God is evident in every one of these biblical examples. Adam and Eve were led out from behind the bushes, clothed, and informed of the coming of their Redeemer (Gen. 3:15). Abraham, in spite of his weaknesses, became the "father of faith" (Rom. 4). The crafty, conniving Jacob was changed in his nature following a bout with an angel and became Israel, the father of a nation set apart unto God (Gen. 32:24–32). Joseph proclaimed to his brothers, "But as for you, ye thought evil against me; but God meant it unto good, to bring to pass, as it is this day, to save much people alive" (Gen. 50:20). Balaam lost a debate with a stubborn donkey (Num. 22:22–34) and David was restored in repentance (II Sam. 12:1–13). Absalom, hanging by his hair from the branch of a tree, died at the hands of a merciless Joab, ending his monarchial ambitions (II Sam 18:14). Haman hung from his own gallows and the Jews triumphed (Esther 7:7–10).

The plotting of the Sanhedrin and the betrayal of Jesus by Judas Iscariot was addressed by Peter in his kerygma, "Him, being delivered by the determinate counsel and foreknowledge of God, ye have taken and by wicked hands have crucified and slain: Whom God hath raised up, having loosed the pains of death: because it was not possible that he should be holden of it" (Acts 2:23, 24). Therefore, " . . . there is none other name under heaven given among men, whereby we must be saved" (Acts 4:12b). The seeming thwarting of Paul's ministry resulted in the writing of nearly half of the New Testament from within the secluded confines of damp first-century dungeons.

Concerns by some Christian writers that an ominous system, like the New Age, could usher in the reign of Antichrist are valid, yet they are easily sensationalized. The biblical record clearly illustrates that we live in a theistic universe, not one left to the conscious, random reordering on a world-wide scale by diabolical coconspirators independent of God's foreordained "plan."

Conclusion

Elliot Miller is very perceptive in setting forth the issue of immediate concern for the Church:

In spite of frequent references to how "freedom of religion" would be an essential feature of the New Age, it is clear from their writings that virtually all New Agers are looking for a spiritually based society. And just as New Age (occult) spirituality is repugnant to, and incompatible with, Christian faith, . . . so orthodox Christianity is repugnant to, and incompatible with, the kind of global society New Agers are working toward. In the New Age there would be no comfortable (more likely nontolerable) place for true Christianity. Christian dogmatism could easily be viewed (in fact, already is) as antievolutionary: a threat to the global unity necessary for racial survival. And when survival dominates over all other values, the elimination of any perceived threat to it could easily be justified.[9]

The particular type of spirituality embraced by the New Age is antagonistic towards Christianity. In fact, New Age mysticism leaves no room for Christianity. Christianity's doctrinal tenets and loyalty to revelation are perceived as barriers to the advanced stage of spiritual awareness promoted by the New Age. However, the Church has been confronted with "lawlessness" from the time of its origin until now as both Scripture and Church history demonstrate.

The radical dualism of many apocalyptic conspiracy theories often breeds paranoia. Unsubstantiated statements about the hidden agenda of the New Age should be avoided. Rather, Christian exposure and resistance of New Age mysticism must be carried out rationally, with biblical wisdom. Satan is a counterfeiter and, therefore, the Christian Church must be discerning, judging wisely, not just according to appearance (John 2:24).

Notes to Chapter 7

1. D. Hicks and D. Lewis, *The Todd Phenomenon* (Harrison, Ark.: New Leaf Press, 1979), pp. 17, 18.

2. William M. Bowen, Jr., *Globalism: America's Demise* (Huntington House, 1984), and Texe Marrs, *Dark Secrets of the New Age* (Crossway Books), are examples of books that set forth themes of a conscious comprehensive conspiracy by the New Age. However, these writers are a basic reproduction of Constance Cumbey's original conspiracy theme.

3. Constance Cumbey, *Hidden Dangers of the Rainbow,* (Shreveport: Huntington House, 1983), p. 90. Alice A. Bailey, *Discipleship in the New Age II* (New York: Lucius Publishing Co., 1955), p. vi, presents "The Great Invocation" also known as the "Plan": From the point of Light within the Mind of God Let the light stream forth into the minds of men. Let the Light descend on Earth. From the point of Love within the Heart of God Let love stream forth into the hearts of men. May Christ return to Earth. From the centre where the Will of God is known Let purpose guide the little wills of men – the purpose which the Masters know and serve. From the centre which we call the

race of men Let the Plan of Love and Light work out And may it seal the door where evil dwells. Let Light and Love and Power restore the Plan on Earth. This invocation is supposed to reveal the hope of the New Age for those of an esoteric or occult tradition. Alice Bailey's works develop this occult theme.

4. See Elliot Miller, *Forward* (San Juan Capistrano: Christian Research Institute, 1983), "Benjamin Creme and The Reappearance of the Christ" for further information on Creme.

5. Cumbey, *The Hidden Dangers of the Rainbow*, p. 90.

6. Alexander, "Plots or Paranoia?" pp. 34, 35.

7. Ibid., p. 35.

8. Elliot Miller, "Saying No to the New Age," *Moody Monthly*, February 1985, p. 22.

9. Elliot Miller, "Tracking The 'Aquarian Conspiracy,' " *Forward*, (San Juan Capistrano: Christian Research Institute, 1987), p. 13.

8 | *To Every New Ager an Answer*

The Apostle Peter exhorts Christians to "Always be prepared to make a defense to any one who calls you to account for the hope that is in you, yet do it with gentleness and reverence" (I Peter 3:15, RSV). The English word "apologetic" is derived from the Greek word, "*apologia*," which is rendered "defense" in this verse. An apologetic is a reasoned defense for one's position or point of view. Therefore, Peter urges Christians to be prepared to defend the Christian faith, to provide answers for why we believe what we believe. Taking his cue from Peter's admonition, C. S. Lewis passionately contends that "We are to defend Christianity itself–the faith preached by the Apostles, attested by the Martyrs, embodied in the Creeds, expounded by the Fathers."[1]

The purpose of this chapter is twofold: (1) to respond apologetically to a sampling of questions often asked of the author during presentations on the New Age; (2) to provide helpful tips for witnessing to individuals within the New Age Movement.

Questions and Answers

The New Age Movement typically claims that the Christian Church believed in reincarnation until the sixth century when Christians suppressed this belief. Please address this accusation.

Reincarnation stands in great contrast to the primary doctrines of the Christian faith. Christianity teaches a once for all sacrifice by Jesus

Christ for the sins of humanity and his triumphal resurrection over death as the means to eternal life, not a hopeless cycle of reincarnations.

The historical reliability of the primary source documents of the Christian faith (chapter six) undercuts this argument. Standing on the infallible rule of Holy Scripture, the Christian Church has condemned reincarnation since its inception. Arguments by the New Age that many early church fathers believed in reincarnation are falsely based on: "(1) a deliberate reconstruction of the evidence which ignores the vast majority of the fathers' testimony; (2) partial quotations of the fathers, usually out of context; (3) interpolations into the quotations from the fathers; and (4) fabricated quotations."[2]

Many of the so-called mystery religions believed in "dying" and "rising" saviors. How is Christianity different from these ancient cults and/or is the Christian faith dependent upon them for its belief in the death and resurrection of the God-man, Jesus Christ?

The early mystery religions of the Mediterranean world include the cults of Demeter and Dionysus, later followed by the Eleusinian and Orphic religions (Greece); the cults of Cybele and Attis flourished in Asia Minor (Phrygia); Isis and Osiris originated in Egypt; the cult of Adonis was present in Syria and Palestine and in Persia, the cult of Mithras thrived.

Christian dependence upon the mystery religions with regard to central Christian doctrines has not been capably demonstrated. Several problems block such efforts: (1) The mythical accounts of dying and rising saviors are non-historical dramas employed as a part of initiation ceremonies. (2) They are vastly different in meaning, purpose, and interpretation from the death and resurrection of Jesus Christ as recorded in the New Testament (for example, the mystery religions do not teach a vicarious death of their saviors. The mystery religions further teach that their saviors die frequently, in accord with the cycles of nature, unlike the once for all death of Jesus Christ, Hebrews 9:25–28). (3) The death of Christ was prophetic, and Jesus died voluntarily, whereas the mythical gods of the mystery religions were either murdered or just overcome by fate. (4) None of the early mystery religions claim that the resurrection of their mythical gods leads to eternal life for the individual who places trust in them. (5) Finally, chronology demonstrates that the mystery religions' teachings about the death and resurrection of their saviors are evolved. Mystery religion sources appealed to in order to demonstrate a Christian dependence are actually post–Christian. This should silence attempts to demonstrate any dependency of Christianity upon the mystery religions.[3]

How can a God, who is both good and omnipotent, allow suffering, particularly of the innocent, within the world?

This question subtly implies a potential dilemma for the Christian faith: Perhaps God is good, but he is unable to fulfill his desire to rid the world of evil, or perhaps he is all powerful and refuses to subdue evil in the world. Which is it? Is God good but not omnipotent or is he omnipotent but an unloving despot?

The problem of evil originated through an irrational world view (Isaiah 14:12–14). Therefore, by nature, evil is irrational. Hence, it indiscriminately strikes both the innocent and the guilty.

The Christian God has demonstrated his goodness by providing sinful man, who originally chose evil in place of the benevolent God (Genesis 3:6; Romans 5:12), a sacrifice for his sin (Romans 5:8). God has further demonstrated his power by raising Christ from the dead for the purpose of reconciling the world unto himself (II Corinthians 5:17–21).

God is *compelled* by his holy nature to carry out justice against sin, but he also chooses, in his own sovereign will, *without obligation*, to have mercy upon all who accept his offer of atonement for their sins through the shed blood of Jesus Christ (John 3:16). Through the cross, both the justice and the mercy of the sovereign God of the universe are awesomely revealed.

Through the life, death, and resurrection of Jesus Christ, God has revealed both his goodness and his power. The Father is patient in waiting for as many as are called to come to the saving knowledge of Jesus Christ (II Peter 3:9). However, Christian eschatology teaches that Christ will return bodily to earth (Acts 1:11; Titus 2:13) in judgment to rid the world of evil and suffering, ultimately revealing his everlasting goodness and glorious power (Revelation 19:6–16; 20:4).

What about atrocities committed by Christians, such as the Christian crusades, the persecution of Jews in the Middle Ages, or the Spanish Inquisition?

Not everything done "in the name of Christ" is of Christ. In other words, it is an injustice to condemn Christianity for the evil activity of some professing Christians when in fact the Bible itself condemns such actions as non-Christian.

John Warwick Montgomery addresses this issue: "Unlike the human rights violations in certain other religious traditions (e.g., discrimination against women and cruel and unusual punishments in Islam), 'Christian' violations of human dignity occur 'in spite of,' not because of, Jesus' teaching. One should judge a belief-system by the acts of its consistent disciples, not those of its inconsistent fellow-travelers."[4]

Without desiring to minimize the significance of this question and the issue it raises, the bumper sticker is quite true that reads: "Christians aren't perfect, just forgiven." Christians are capable of sinning, like everyone else, and this they certainly do. The Christian faith does not teach that Christians will reach moral perfection in this life; therefore, Christians must trust daily in the continual cleansing of Christ's blood of their sins (I John 1:9-10).

The sins of Christians are "their own, and ought not be attributed to the One who saves them by his acts of grace and love. The gospel and the Scriptures remain the answer to man's ultimate human rights dilemmas, whether or not the human race—or the church itself—follows the revelation given to it."[5]

Christianity has been around for almost 2000 years, and yet the world is presently in great despair—war, famine, pestilence, racism, and hatred fill the earth. Doesn't this reveal Christianity's failure and argue the need for a new solution to the world's problems?

First of all, this question ignores the sinfulness of man's nature. Man is culpable, because of sin, of violence, hate, greed, selfishness, murder, theft, torture, terrorism, etc. These things affirm the testimony of Scripture concerning the nature of man (Romans 1:18-32; II Timothy 3:1-8). Mankind desperately needs a Savior, and Jesus Christ has come into the world, not to condemn the world, but to bring salvation to all who trust in his Name (John 3:17) and to destroy the evil works of the Devil (I John 3:8).

Secondly, the Christian Church needs to humbly come before God in repentance. God's people are called to repentance so that God will again turn his face towards our land and heal it (II Chronicles 7:14).

We need reformation, revival, and constructive revolution within the Christian Church today. The Church is called to be the prophetic conscience for culture. The negligence of the Church has resulted in excesses within our culture. Instead of mocking a New Ager or uncontrollably blasting him for plotting to enthrone the Antichrist, Christians need to repent before God and ask this generation to forgive us for our failure to minister to them the whole counsel of God! The world doesn't need the empty, pernicious myth of the New Age leading to a mind-bending transformation. It needs the unadulterated gospel of the risen Savior and Lord Jesus Christ.

Wherever the gospel is preached it gives rise to science, great educational institutions, hospitals, welfare systems, human rights, and human dignity. The Church needs to return from the fringes of culture, to the center of culture, and once again act as its prophetic conscience.

Francis Schaeffer contends: "He is the same God, he is the living God, he is the unchanging God. He is the God who is there. And will he not do in the midst of this situation what he did in the midst of the Jewish situation in the time of Isaiah in the Northern Kingdom, and in the time of Jeremiah and Ezekiel and Daniel in the Southern Kingdom? Will he not judge our culture? Will he not call it adulterous? I tell you in the name of God he will judge our culture, and he 'is' judging our culture."[6] The Church is presently on the verge of turning our culture over to the ungodly by default.

What about the hypocrisy within the Church?

This question is related to the two previous questions and therefore, I will not elaborate in answering it. Suffice it to say that I do not place my trust in the Church for eternal life, but rather in Jesus Christ. This is not to minimize the significance of the Church. The Church is the Body of Christ and contrary to the rationalizations of some, faithfulness to the local church is a visible witness for Christ for the sake of encouraging one another, for the sake of spiritual growth, and for the sake of bringing others who do not know Christ into the Body of Christ. In this way we impact the lives of others and the entire community and do so in obedience to his Word (Hebrews 10:25). Jesus Christ is not a hypocrite. However, you are a hypocrite if you profess to be one of his and yet, you are not obedient to his Word.

Please comment on Benjamin Creme's disillusionment, among other New Age leaders, with Christianity's presentation of "a picture of the Christ impossible for the majority of thinking people today to accept—as the One and Only

Son of God, sacrificed by his Loving Father to save Humanity from the results of its sins; as a Blood Sacrifice straight out of the old and outworn Jewish Dispensation."[7]

Truth, according to Benjamin Creme in specific and the New Age in general, is subjective and relative. Christianity understands truth to be transcendent, founded upon the very character of God and therefore absolute.

The resurrection of Jesus Christ points to the objective God "who is there" and who has propositionally spoken to man. The self-disclosure of the living God to man (i.e., the Bible) requires all men everywhere to repent of their sins and turn to God through Jesus Christ. Since this is objective, absolute truth, it matters little what Benjamin Creme, myself, or anyone else really thinks; what matters is what the everlasting God of truth thinks. God's revelation, instead of the superstitious imagination of men like Benjamin Creme, is a sure foundation for truth.

It should be further pointed out that many people in our culture understand Christianity in terms of a descriptive definition. A descriptive definition is based upon how they see certain Christians behave or how they may have been treated by Christians. From these experiences, they define Christianity. In a good majority of the cases, they define Christianity in negative terms. A normative definition of Christianity defines Christianity in accord with the Scriptures. Regardless of the failures of men, Christianity must be defined and understood in terms of the Bible, particularly the New Testament, and not in terms of a prejudiced, descriptive definition. I cannot stress this point too strongly.[8]

How do you explain the presence of Christian themes in myths and fairy tales?

John Warwick Montgomery explains that, "man is fundamentally mythic. His real health depends upon his knowing and living his metaphysical totality. In myth man discovers and affirms not his disparate nature but his mythic, his archetypal and cosmic nature."[9] Myths and fairy tales represent man's desire to be in harmony with his world, his fellowman, and God.

Thomas Aquinas, the great Catholic theologian from the thirteenth century, noted, in concert with Scripture, that no man seeks after God (Romans 3:10–12). Aquinas further observed that men therefore desire the benefits of knowing the only true God without having to know him. Myths and fairy tales often engage man with the great Christian themes without the requirement of picking up their cross and making him Lord of their lives, instead of themselves.

Many cults, such as the Mormons, and world religions, such as Islam, claim that God has revealed to them a higher revelation beyond the Old and New Testaments. How do we answer this claim?

I personally believe that the canon of the Bible is closed (Hebrews 1:1–3). However, if God did want to give further revelation, then a sovereign God is certainly free to do so!

However, the historical reliability of the Bible is an irrefutable fact (see chapter six). Further, the Bible reveals an unchanging God (Malachi 3:6). The God of the Bible is therefore consistent in truth. God would therefore not communicate to one generation and then contradict himself to the next. For example, since the Bible antedates both the Book of Mormon and the Koran, then they must conform to the Bible, not the other way around. Not only are these two alleged "revelations" historically unreliable, they contradict the Bible in several places. If God is consistent in truth, then both Mormonism and Islam are false (also applied to New Age claims of esoteric "revelations" such as *A Course In Miracles*, etc.).

The presence of so many Christian denominations is not only confusing, but further indicates that there is more division and strife than agreement as to what is true in Christianity.

In his book, *The Church Before the Watching World*, Francis Schaeffer speaks of Christianity as a circle, rather than a point. Within the circle, there is room to move. At the center of the circle the primary doctrines of the Christian faith (e.g., virgin birth, deity of Christ, the trinity, blood atonement, salvation by faith alone, the bodily resurrection of Christ, the ascension and priestly ministry of Christ, the visible return of Christ) provide the basis for unity among all Christian denominations, whether they be Lutheran, Presbyterian, Baptist, Assemblies of God, Free Methodist. Moving out from the center of the circle, modes of baptism (i.e., sprinkling or immersion), worship style, spiritual gifts, ritual and ceremonialism, and other denominational distinctives are encountered. The diversity that exists as one moves toward the boundaries is anchored in unity at the heart of the circle. "Yet if one goes too far, he falls off the cliff on the other side" into the abyss of heresy and spiritual delusion.[10] There is tolerance within the Christian community, leading to diversity. Yet, the Christian Church has historically been intolerant of perversions of the gospel, for it is the message of salvation freely offered to all mankind (Galatians 1:6–9; 3:13).

How can a Christian be both a sinner and justified before God?

The Reformers proclaimed that Christians are "simul justi et peccatores": sinners and justified at the same time. As the sovereign God calls men to repentance of their sin, He draws them to the Christ (John 6:44), imputing the righteousness of Christ to sinful man (Romans 4:22–25) and thereby declaring him just (Romans 8:30). Because of the righteousness of Jesus Christ, an individual is just before God (II Corinthians 5:17–21) in his vertical relationship with God. Paradoxically, man still wrestles with a fallen nature in his horizonal life (earthly, existential daily life) requiring sanctification to take place in his life (Romans 6 & 7). The blood of Christ acts as a propitiation (covering) for an individual's sin, keeping him in fellowship with the living God by sheer grace (I John 1:8–10).

Karl Marx referred to religion as the "opiate of the masses," and Sigmund Freud ascribes religion to psychosis. How does the Christian defend the faith against these widespread views?

Karl Marx and Sigmund Freud were not original thinkers in their attacks upon religion, particularly Christianity. Ludwig Feuerbach, "the classical skeptic in theology," authored the illusionary theory of religion, positing that God is merely a projection of man's own ego, a wish fulfillment. Feuerbach's principal works are *The Essence of Christianity* (1841), *The Philosophy of the Future* (1843), and *The Essence of Religion* (1853). He died in 1872.

Eduard von Hartmann, "the philosopher of pessimism," observes four major flaws in Feuerbach's attacks upon religion: (1) His argument is founded upon a simple fallacy: "To call God a wish-fulfillment is in one sense a statement which has no bearing of any kind on the question of his reality or unreality. It simply admonishes us to use special care in scrutinizing the evidence for and against." (2) "Feuerbach, like the colour-blind, is apt to conclude that what he does not see is not there." He has no grounds to disclaim the personal subjective experience of another individual. (3) Feuerbach succumbs to solipsism, the view that only what one senses himself is realistic. This view not only attacks the existence of God, it makes all knowledge suspect. Thus Feuerbach undermines his own arguments through epistemological suicide. (4) Finally, Feuerbach ignores death and the reality of sin.[11]

R. C. Sproul astutely observes that "The problem is not that there is insufficient evidence to convince rational beings that there is a God, but that rational beings have a natural antipathy to the being of God. In a word, the nature of God (at least the Christian God) is 'repugnant' to man and is not the focus of desire or wish-projection. Man's desire is not that Yahweh exists, but that He doesn't. The New Testament sees not only atheism but human fabricated religion as being grounded in such antipathy."[12]

How do we know what the canon of the New Testament should be?

The term "canon" means rule or standard and carries the thought of authority. The Church has not established the canon, but rather it has discovered the canon. The New Testament canon is characterized by five distinctive traits that portray a book's divine origin: (1) authoritative nature; (2) prophetic content; (3) authenticity; (4) dynamic nature; and (5) acceptance.

The authority of a book refers to its compatibility with the rest of the canon as to internal consistency, focus of doctrine, and infallibility of content. The prophetic content of a book is not only the demonstration of the fulfillment of predictive prophecy, but also its thematic compatibility with the Old Testament relative to the nature and character of God. The authenticity of a book refers to its authorship. In the case of the New Testament, was it written by an apostle or a close associate of an apostle? The dynamism of a book involves its ability to impact human lives in a life-changing manner. Finally, the acceptance of a book refers to the approval of that book by the universal Christian community.

The ultimate test of any book of the canon is its testimony of the Savior through its focus upon the primary doctrines of the Christian faith as established upon the person, nature and work of the Lord Jesus Christ.

The New Age refers to Jesus Christ in a reverential manner. Doesn't this demonstrate a compatibility with Christianity?

"Whom do men say that I the Son of man am?" asked Jesus of his disciples. The disciples responded, "Some say that thou art John the Baptist: some, Elias; and others, Jeremias, or one of the prophets" (Matthew 16:13–14, KJV).

Already, in the first century, men held different opinions concerning who Jesus Christ is. The twentieth century is no different. To the Mormons, Jesus is the illegitimate offspring of a resurrected, glorified man who turns out to be Adam in the teaching of Brigham Young. To the Jehovah's Witnesses, Jesus is the first and greatest creation of Jehovah God, who rose from the dead spiritually (not bodily) and invisibly return to Brooklyn, New York, in 1914 to set up his earthly headquarters! To the Unification Church (Moonies), he is a failure, having been crucified before he could fulfill his earthly mission. Now the world must look for the "Lord of the Second Advent," which is none other than Sun Myung Moon. To the Spiritists, he is a medium in the sixth-sphere of astral projection, and in the teachings of Mary Baker Eddy (Christian Science), he is a divine idea. The Unitarian Church claims that Jesus was a very good man mistakenly deified by his followers, and the Church Universal and Triumphant places Jesus among their pantheon of ascended masters, stripped of his uniqueness as Lord and Savior.

These are but a few examples of what the Apostle Paul referred to as "another Jesus" (II Corinthians 11:4). So it is with the New Age which professes Jesus as merely one of a long line of avatars (Hindu term for manifestation of the impersonal god in man) who has come into the world to point men towards enlightenment. Instead of the only way unto the Father (John 14:6), the New Age Jesus is one of many ways. The Christ, considered separate from Jesus, is identified with the consciousness of the world, cast in the pantheistic mode of the New Age.

In First John, the Apostle provides the Christian with discernment concerning "another Jesus." The Apostle informs us that these are the last days and "as ye have heard that antichrist shall come, even now are there many antichrists; whereby we know that it is the last time" (2:18). The Greek word used here for "antichrist" is a compound word. *Christos* (Christ) means the anointed One, and the preposition *anti* here means, in the place of (*Thayer's Greek-English Lexicon of the New Testament*, p. 49, 2.). Both the antichrist and the antichrists share in common "the spirit of antichrist" (4:3). The purpose of the spirit of antichrist is summed up in its name: To replace the Christ of Scripture with another, a counterfeit Christ.

The Jesus of the New Age is "another Jesus," not the Jesus of biblical revelation. The Jesus of the Bible is God incarnate (John 1:1, 14) and the Jesus of the New Age is a pantheistic imposter.

How can man have a free moral will in a universe lorded over by a Sovereign God?

Often, this question originates in a person's mind as the result of a confusion of the concepts of autonomy and free will. When we speak of autonomy, this refers to man's absolute freedom without regard to an infinite God. Man is lord of his own life and he is in control of his own ultimate destiny. Free will refers to a limited freedom of mankind. Man's freedom is limited by God's sovereignty. God, however, does not deny our free moral choice. Quite the contrary. In the Christian tradition, man is very wonderfully created in the image of God and because of his special creation, man possesses inherent dignity (Genesis 1:26; Psalm 8) and personal freedom.

We have the ability to make moral choices, and yet, God will interweave all of our choices into his grand plan for our lives, resulting in his ultimate, providential control of our lives (Romans 8:28). Only a loving, caring, Sovereign God could provide man with such ultimate purpose for his life.

Should Christians avoid all holistic health practices?

A medical emphasis upon the whole person is not only healthy, but biblical and often lacking in our society. The problem is not with a holistic concept of man, it is with the world view of oneness that many holistic health practitioners attempt to orientate the patient to, resulting in the uncritical acceptance of New Age pantheism.

A second point to be made here is that the New Age, whether its therapies work or not, has reduced religion to therapy. A religion that offers nothing more than a sense of well-being or a spiritual high is like another drug in our drug-ridden society.

Christians who may consider holistic health as an alternative to conventional medicine should critically put the methodologies of the practitioner to the test of biblical revelation (I Thessalonians 5:21).

What does the rainbow mean in the New Age and should I not display one as a Christian?

To the New Age, the rainbow represents the peace and tranquility on the earth that will follow this present era of global tragedy. The rainbow is also the sign of the Noahic covenant, the promise from God to Noah that he would not again destroy the earth with a worldwide flood (Genesis 9:8–15).

Since the rainbow is a part of God's covenant with Noah, Christians should feel free to display rainbows. The use of the rainbow by the New Age should in no wise deter a Christian from remembering the covenants of their God with mankind.

In an effort to refute the resurrection, many have theorized that Jesus did not actually die on the cross.

If Jesus of Nazareth did not actually die on the cross, then there was no supernatural resurrection and the faith of the Christian is hopeless vanity (I Corinthians 15:14).

First of all, I have already demonstrated the reliability of the primary source documents that record his death as a fact by eyewitnesses (Matthew 27:50; Mark 15:37; Luke 23:46; John 19:30). Secondly, theories such as the resuscitation theory (also known as the swoon theory) are reduced to absurdity when we are asked to believe that, half dead due to blood loss, a beating, and no medical attention after his crucifixion, Jesus struggled free from his shroud, pushed aside a stone that three healthy women were not sure they could move (see Mark 16:3), and walked several miles on wounded feet. Then he met his disciples, claimed to be risen, victorious over the power of death, and was so convincing that Thomas called him "My Lord and my God" (John 20:28). After about a month he wandered off and died in solitude. No one ever found his body. This is a theory of last resort. A supernatural resurrection is certainly not less probable than this, unless we reject it from the outset."[13]

William Edwards, a Mayo Clinic pathologist, and his colleagues report in the *Journal of the American Medical Association* that the spear of the Roman soldier, thrust into Jesus' side (John 19:34), probably released clear lung fluid just prior to piercing the right ventricle of the heart of Christ. Edwards and his colleagues conclude that Christ was dead before this act by the Roman soldier.

In a detailed report on the Romans' excruciating method of execution, known as crucifixion, Edwards emphasizes the state of shock incurred from trauma and significant blood loss from the severe flogging suffered by Jesus and the great difficulty of breathing on the cross. "The full weight of the body pulled down on a victim's wrists (not the palms), which were nailed to the crossbar. If he tried to relieve the pressure by straightening up, his body weight pushed down on his feet, nailed to the vertical post. The painful position necessitated shallow exhalation, which led to a buildup of carbon dioxide in the blood and eventual asphyxia. Cardiac rupture could also have been involved."[14] Edwards and his colleagues firmly concluded that "Christ did die on the cross—his purported resurrection can't be attributed to physical resuscitation."[15]

Witnessing to the New Age

Following my presentation on the New Age, a pastor's wife approached to tell me about an experience she had had while flying cross-country. She sat beside a New Age enthusiast for the entire trip. Shortly into the flight, she engaged the man in conversation and sought for an opportunity to introduce Jesus Christ into their dialogue. Before she had this opportunity, the man began to talk to her about his many spiritual odysseys in the New Age Movement.

The pastor's wife began to expound upon the fact that the man did not need his occult experiences, he rather needed to be born again following a commitment to Jesus Christ. To this, the man replied that she was ignorant and needed to be enlightened. As each one of them contended for the validity of their own subjective experience, the friendly skies were spanned and the trip came to an end with neither the pastor's wife or the New Age mystic being persuaded. The experience of the pastor's wife reveals some potential frustrations when we attempt to witness to the New Age mystic.

Os Guinness makes a significant point in this regard: " 'That' God is, is no problem. It is 'Who' God is that is the crux of their conversion."[16] The point here is, don't argue about experience with the New Age mystic, you will quickly discover, as did the pastor's wife, that this is like trying to play handball in a field!

The primary objective of your witness to the New Ager should be to direct them to the One who has shown us who God is—Jesus Christ (John 14:9). An effective way of accomplishing this is as follows:

1. The New Ager is under spiritual delusion as a result of rejecting the truth in favor of occult mysticism (II Thessalonians 2:10–11). Christian love penetrates the spiritual delusion of the New Ager. Therefore, approach the New Age mystic patiently, grounded in the love of God. If the New Ager feels that they are an object of antagonism because they are an enemy of the Cross, then you will miss any opportunity for personal identification. Identify with the New Ager as a person, created in the image of God and therefore of great worth to God and to you. In laboring patiently, exhaustively, and prayerfully with the New Ager, you will preserve their dignity and win their respect.

2. Always keep in focus that your primary goal is not to win an argument but rather a soul through the presentation of the gospel in a way that is understandable for the New Ager.

3. When you do win an argument on a given point with the New Ager, don't immediately go for the jugular. Back off and seize the opportunity to reinforce a "we" situation, avoiding an "us" and "you" situation. In other words, seek to establish a common ground with the New Ager. Let them know that you respect their search for meaning in life and you, too, desire a sense of meaning and purpose in life. There are a number of other areas, common to all thinking and sensitive people, that cross between Christians and New Agers; for example, ecological concerns, overpopulation, human dignity, human potential (short of unlimited human potential, it should be emphasized that the Christian world view stresses human development), world peace, hunger, and especially, a future new era for humanity.

Obviously, the point of departure with the New Age is the grand Christian solution to world crisis; however, seeking common ground with the New Ager will provide a starting point for you to introduce Jesus Christ as the grand solution to the human situation.

4. Insure that the New Ager understands Christianity in terms of a normative definition (as defined by the New Testament) instead of a descriptive definition (as based on personal observation of the behavior of some Christians, usually poor examples). This step is extremely important and often results in the New Ager actually hearing the gos-

pel clearly presented for the first time in their lives. By way of suggestion, begin with: I Corinthians 15:1–4.

In presenting the gospel to the New Ager, seek opportunities to use terms common to both Christianity and the New Age (e.g., use "separation," "transformation," for "born again"). Introducing familiar-sounding terms to the New Ager within a scriptural context will greatly aid your witness. For example, because we are separated from God because of sin (Romans 3:23), we need the transforming power of the Holy Spirit (2 Corinthians 5:17; Romans 12:2; Titus 3:5), so that we can come into personal relationship with God through Jesus Christ (Hebrews 7:25).

5. Practice what the late Walter Martin often referred to as "Rabbinic rhetoric" in your witness. Rabbinic rhetoric involves asking the New Ager questions concerning the Christian faith and the New Age in such a way that you bring him to a point of objective evaluation of his position (this is very important because for the New Ager, truth is only subjective) and you allow the Word of God to minister to them in terms that they discover truth themselves instead of feeling preached into a corner.

6. Define terms for the understanding of both yourself and the New Ager. The importance of this is inestimable. Without a definition of terms, communication with the New Ager will be fruitless. Words mean what they mean by definition, context, and common usage. New Agers often understand Christian vocabulary in entirely different terms than do Christians. Additionally, understand the use of certain terms by the New Ager.

7. As a part of evangelizing the New Age, be prepared to give answers (apologetics) for your faith in Jesus Christ.

You will lose the respect of the New Ager if he does not perceive that you are interested in his questions. The Christian Church has often been guilty of answering questions that no one is asking in our contemporary society. Be attentive and concerned with exactly what is on the New Ager's mind.

If you don't know the answer to a New Ager's question, tell them so and make arrangements to contact them later with an answer. Do not skirt the issue as though it is of no importance.

8. Avoid attacking the fringe elements of the New Age (e.g., the antics of Shirley MacLaine, fire-walking, crystals, etc.). Concentrate on

the main issues (e.g., planetary survival, the New Age world view, life after death, and salvation).

9. Keep the issue of objective truth constantly in focus. The New Ager thinks in terms of relativism and therefore dissociates himself from the notion of an ultimate reality outside of himself. This is because of his pantheistic world view. The point must be made that the true Christian has made an unconditional commitment to Jesus Christ because Christianity is objectively true.

10. Finally, regardless of the attitude of the New Ager or your own frustration, always remember that Jesus Christ "is the propitiation for our sins: and not for our's only, but also for the sins of the whole world" (I John 2:2).

In conclusion, Douglas Groothuis provides wise insight: "If we only separate from and condemn evil, we become merely reactionary— more anti-New Age than pro-Christ. Our constructive values—inasmuch as we develop them at all—take a back seat to our critical evaluations. And instead of seeking first the kingdom of God, we seek first to expose the kingdom of evil. As a result, our demonology may become more developed than our Christology."[17]

Notes to Chapter 8

1. C. S. Lewis, *God in the Dock*, p. 90.
2. Joseph P. Gudel, Robert M. Bowman, Jr., and Dan R. Schlesinger, "Reincarnation—Did the Church Suppress It?" *Christian Research Journal*, Summer 1987, p. 9. This article is an excellent treatment of the claim that the Church suppressed belief in reincarnation in the sixth century. For a copy of this journal, write: Christian Research Institute, P.O. Box 500, San Juan Capistrano, Calif. 92693. Also see: Mark Albrecht, *Reincarnation: A Christian Appraisal* (Downers Grove: InterVarsity Press, 1982); Norman Geisler and J. Yutaka Amano, *The Reincarnation Sensation* (Wheaton: Tyndale House Publishers, 1986), and Martin, *The New Cults*.
3. Ronald H. Nash, *Christianity & the Hellenistic World* (Grand Rapids: Zondervan, 1984), p. 195. Nash's book is an excellent, in-depth treatment of this subject matter. Nash cautions against three common pitfalls inherent in efforts to demonstrate the dependence of Christianity upon the mystery religions: "First, we must distinguish between early and later forms of the mystery religions. Second, we must avoid the assumption that just because a cult had a certain belief or practice in the third or fourth century, it therefore had the same belief or practice in the first century. Third, we must avoid any indiscriminate conjoining of facts from different centuries. The relatively late information we

have about the pagan religions should not uncritically be read back into earlier stages in their development."

4. John Warwick Montgomery, *Human Rights & Human Dignity* (Grand Rapids: Zondervan, 1986), p. 185.

5. Ibid., pp. 185–86.

6. Francis A. Schaeffer, *The Church before the Watching World* (Downers Grove: InterVarsity Press, 1971), p. 57.

7. Creme, *The Reappearance of the Christ and the Masters of Wisdom*, p. 25.

8. See C. S. Lewis, *God in the Dock*, chapter 10, "Christian Apologetics," for an interesting discussion on this crucial issue.

9. John Warwick Montgomery, ed., *Myth, Allegory and Gospel* (Minneapolis: Bethany Fellowship, Inc., 1974), p. 121. This book is an interpretation of the works of J. R. R. Tolkien, C. S. Lewis, G. K. Chesterton, and Charles Williams. It is a unique and insightful study in this particular area of concern.

10. Schaeffer, *The Church Before the Watching World*, p. 93.

11. H. R. Mackintosh, *Types of Modern Theology*, "The Negative Development in Strauss and Feuerbach," pp. 126–27.

12. R. C. Sproul, *If There Is a God, Why Are There Atheists?* (Minneapolis: Bethany House, 1978), pp. 56–57.

13. Gordon Carkner, Herbert Gruning, J. Richard Middleton, and Bruce Toombs, *Ten Myths About Christianity*, published by the authors, August 1984, p. 9.

14. *Science Digest*, "New Science," August 1986, p. 14.

15. Ibid. Also see McDowell, *The Resurrection Factor*, chapters 5 and 6, for an excellent study of and refutation of several fallacious theories advanced in an attempt to refute the resurrection by denying the Jesus actually died by crucifixion.

16. Guinness, *The Dust of Death*, p. 301.

17. Douglas Groothuis, "Confronting The New Age," *Christianity Today*, January 13, 1989, p. 37.

Appendix

Christian Perspectives and Antidotes

Our pluralistic society is characterized by relativistic winds of thought. A condition of social pluralism, as sociologists observe, is a temporary condition. Pluralism is a cultural bridge from a former predominant world view to a new prevailing world view.

The New Age Myth is tirelessly working to usurp the prophetic role of the Christian Church in "post–Christian" Western civilization. Based upon a new way of understanding the present, the New Age is calling for a new way of looking at Western civilization's future. The New Myth is subtly weaving its deceitful web throughout our culture (e.g., business, education, politics, science, medicine, and even religion).

Whereas the Christian Church tends to be more supportive of traditional values and established social institutions, the New Age is answering society's desperate cry for change. Elliot Miller is very insightful in this regard:

> Because our faith has been historically embraced by the cultural establishment, we are readily disposed to expend our efforts upholding or defending the traditional (a worthy endeavor, when the traditional is also biblical). But we are less inclined to concern ourselves finding biblically acceptable solutions to the most strongly felt needs created by our rapidly changing society.

New Agers, on the other hand, do not perceive themselves tied to the established system. They feel that a new system is needed. So they are more disposed to be "innovators," developing alternatives to inadequate or outmoded social structures.[1]

Over the past three decades, in the name of the separation of church and state, the Church has been shoved to the fringes of culture and replaced by secularism. The Church has actually encouraged this prophetic shift by assuming the identity of Jonah, the ancient Jewish prophet.

Jonah was called by God to preach repentance to the people of Nineveh, a great Syrian city and pagan center. In rejecting God's call, Jonah ironically decided to flee to another pagan capital, Tarshish. After paying his sailing fee, the prophet set sail with the rest of the ship's company to Tarshish.

The Lord, however, was intolerant of Jonah's disobedience and "sent a great wind on the sea, and such a violent storm arose that the ship threatened to break up" (Jonah 1:4, NIV). The terrified sailors began to cry out to their gods and tried to save the ship by throwing the cargo overboard in order to lighten the load. Somehow, Jonah was able to sleep through much of the storm!

Finally, the crew realized that they were about to pay for Jonah's disobedience with their own lives. After casting lots to "find out who is responsible for this calamity" (Jonah 1:7, NIV) they went to Jonah and asked him what they could do to calm the sea. Jonah admitted that he was the cause of their distress. The prophet suggested that the crew cast him overboard, and they obliged. The sea calmed around the ship and the God-fearing, repentant, bobbing prophet.

The New Age is a storm sent by the sovereign God of the universe to awaken his Church in these final hours of human history to the desperation of the lost who are facing a Christless eternity. Douglas Groothuis's plea is noteworthy: "We ought to shed a little light instead of simply cursing the darkness."[2]

The Church needs reformation that will impact society once again with Christian values, social innovations, and prophetic conquest of our dying culture. The Church's flight to its own Tarshish, confusing godly separation with isolationism, is resulting in the turning over of our culture to the ungodly by default. To simply curse the darkness may very possibly be defying the purposes of the living God for his Church.

Human Potential Seminars

The self-deifying themes of the human potential movement are being marketed in a variety of settings, including churches, schools, military bases, prisons, police and fire departments. "Growth" seminars are designed to undermine and replace the existing belief systems of individuals with New Age ideology. Much of this is accomplished through the use of "transformational technologies" by psychospiritual groups like the Forum, Lifespring, Silva Mind Control, and Esalen Institute. Other techniques include meditation, guided imagery, self-hypnosis, therapeutic touch, biofeedback, yoga, and fire-walking.

The union of karma and capitalism produces greater productivity, better relational skills, and individual success, according to promoters of the New Age human potential seminars. Corporations seeking capital bliss are easily caught in the web of New Age networks.

Seizing upon our culture's ignorance of the distinctive nature of religion, New Agers are making significant inroads into schools as well. Promising to improve learning skills through critical thinking, personal awareness, and improved behavior, frustrated administrators and teachers have welcomed New Age educational techniques and training with open arms into the classrooms.

If Western civilization will not go to the ashram, the New Age will bring the ashram to Western civilization. Beginning with the basic assumptions that humans are naturally good and that personal awareness is a valid pursuit of the individual, the New Myth seeks to inform the masses of their unlimited human potential by masking religion in psychological terms.

Christian Resistance

Christian resistance would be wise in avoiding emotional, reactionary, oversimplifications. The Christian ethic, as revealed in Scripture, provides the rationale for Christians to address such matters as human rights violations, hunger, homelessness, environmental concerns, political unrest, health care, educational reform. Western Christianity needs to experience another great reformation, resulting in the restoration of a consistent biblical world and life view. The dynamic transformation of the world has been historically realized through reformation, revival, and constructive revolution within the Church. Christians, not New Agers, are called to repentance and to seek God's face so that he, in his sovereign will, might turn again to our land and bring healing to it (II Chronicles 7:14).

Charles Colson establishes four convictions for the Christian community in its calling to take the gospel to "Nineveh":

(1) Restore orthodoxy. Live by the laws of God's kingdom and Jesus' teachings of Christian truth. Fundamental, basic beliefs are necessary (2 Thess. 2:15). To preach that if you come to God he'll give you anything you want is to preach a false gospel. Lose orthodoxy and you lose the heart of the church.

(2) "Be" the church; it is the community of the redeemed. Be God's people. Make Jesus Lord.

(3) Think and, therefore, act like Christians. Apply the truth of Scripture in the marketplace. Argue every principle of life from this perspective: "current events in the eyes of God."

(4) Confess the faith. Be the salt and the light—take the Good News to others so they may understand the gospel and glorify God (Matt. 5:13-16).[3]

The U.S. Supreme Court has determined that religion refers to beliefs that address the nature of man, his place in the universe, and his relationship to "ultimate" reality. For discerning the religious nature of a particular ideology, Jacob Needleman provides five suggestions:

1. What does it say about man's existential situation, his place in the universe and relationship to God?

2. What does it promise?

3. What does it demand?

4. What sort of people does it attract and what have they experienced?

5. Who are the leaders and what sort of people are they?[4]

Sharon Fish adds four additional questions to Needleman's list:

6. What are the underlying assumptions about the nature of God, man, and the universe?

7. What does it say about sin and the solution to sin?

8. What does it teach about the means of establishing a relationship with God?

9. What is the ultimate aim or end or this teaching?[5]

The exposure of religious teachings or practices is on very dangerous ground constitutionally. A Christian whose employer is requiring him to attend a New Age human potential seminar has the legal right under Title 7 (Theory of Religious Accommodation) to not only refuse to participate in the seminar, but to also request an alternative program for himself and others who feel that their religious convictions are being imposed upon.

Robert Burrows provides some general guidelines for discerning New Age influences: "avoid programs, workshops, seminars, and therapies that (1) are explained in terms of harmonizing, manipulating, integrating, or balancing energies or polarities; (2) denigrate the value of the mind and belief; and (3) make extravagant claims—if it seems too good to be true, it probably is."[6]

Within the public school setting, Christians can respond to New Age influences in a number of ways.

1. Christian educators can contribute to educational reforms by offering innovative ideas that emphasize positive approaches to education and yet reject the religious base of New Age curriculums.

2. Parents need to attend school board meetings and conferences with teachers in order to be informed about what their child is being taught.

3. If parents object to the content of teaching materials in their child's school, they need to protest to administrators and expose the New Age influences within the curriculums.

4. In exposing New Age influences, avoid appealing to Scripture or Christian values directly. Those pledging allegiance to the secular world are not only unsympathetic and ignorant of your Christian convictions, they will immediately interpret your appeal as a "fundamentalist reaction" to positive changes in the educational process. They will further conclude, in many cases, that you are actually trying to impose Christianity upon the school's curricula instead of exposing the religious subtleties of the New Age.

Although your concern is born out of your Christian convictions, seek common constitutional ground with the public schools. In this manner, Christians will serve their purposes to the greatest extent.

5. Avoid requiring others (i.e., the Church, Christian schools) to teach your child Christian values. At a very early age, a child begins to learn and practice values. It is your responsibility to "Train up a child

in the way he should go: and when he is old, he will not depart from it" (Proverbs 22:6). There is no adequate substitute for you where your child is concerned. Be sensitive to your child's questions concerning the Christian faith and insure that you make every effort to answer your child's questions instead of referring them to someone else.

6. Since public schools are just that, public, they are concerned with the consensus of the communities that they serve. Therefore, enlist the testimony of other church members, friends, neighbors, and relatives in protesting the influence of Eastern religious concepts upon the school curricula.

Conclusion

Instead of an isolationist mentality, Christians need to infiltrate all areas of culture and demonstrate in prophetic and creative ways the relevancy of the Christian faith.

Much of the Western Church is characterized by secular thinking. A reformation leading to a renewed commitment to the Judeo-Christian world view must follow the jettison of secular thinking within the Church.

On a national and local level, each Christian is called to bring a Christian perspective to the surrounding culture (Matthew 5:13). Elliot Miller correctly concludes that "The bottom line is that if we want Western society to move once again in a Christian direction, we have to be willing to get more (redemptively) 'involved' in society."[7]

The current global crisis is a reality. If the Christian Church fails to address contemporary world concerns, the New Age (or another competing world view) will shape the thinking of masses of people. God forbid that the Church should be caught sleeping through the storm and the solemn words of Jesus Christ become a tragic reality: "Nevertheless when the Son of man cometh, shall he find faith on the earth?" (Luke 18:8).

Notes to Appendix

1. Elliot Miller, "Tracking the Aquarian Conspiracy," *Christian Research Journal*, Winter/Spring 1987, p. 17.
2. Groothuis, "Confronting the New Age," p. 36.

3. Chuck Colson, Christian Booksellers' Association Convention, Anaheim, Calif., 12 July 1987; idem, El Montecito Presbyterian Church, Santa Barbara, Calif., 18 October 1987. Quoted in Russell Chandler, *Understanding the New Age* (Dallas: Word Publishing, 1988), pp. 303–4.

4. Jacob Needleman, *The New Religions* (New York: E. P. Dutton & Co., 1977), p. 10. Quoted by Sharon Fish, "Holistic Health and the Nursing Profession," *SCP Journal*, August, 1978, p. 41.

5. Fish, ibid., p. 41.

6. Robert Burrows, "New Age Movement: Self-Deification in a Secular Culture," *SCP Newsletter*, Winter 1984–85, p. 4.

7. Miller, "Tracking the Aquarian Conspiracy," p. 17.

Glossary

Acupuncture. This holistic health technique defines disease in terms of an imbalance in "energy flow." Needles are inserted in the body at key points to redirect the energy flow and bring restored balance to the holistic nature of man. Acupuncture has its roots in Chinese medicine and philosophy.

Akashic Records. Records containing all knowledge as recorded by the "Universal Mind." These mysterious records exist in the occultic ethereal realm.

Alchemy. One of the oldest occult sciences known to man. Alchemy has its roots in chemistry. Material elements are believed to be lower forms than spiritual realities. Alchemy teaches a pantheistic world view emphasizing that the Universal Consciousness is manifested in innumerable forms.

Ascended Master. A spiritual entity that has been released from the cycles of reincarnation to occupy a heavenly status and aid men in their evolutionary development.

Astral Body. The spiritual, non-material body possessed by all humans. This spiritual body continues to exist after death according to occultists.

Astral Projection. Refers to out-of-body experiences. During out-of-body experiences, the astral and physical bodies are believed to remain connected by a "silver cord."

Astrology. A belief system asserting that human lives are controlled to a large degree by the positions of the planets and stars.

Atman. Hindu term for the soul of man. The atman is considered divine.

Attunement. The mystical sense of oneness with the microcosm (man) and the macrocosm (cosmos). Synonym for at-one-ment.

Aura.   A psychic energy field claimed by occultists to emanate from all living creatures and special inanimate objects.

Avatar.   A manifestation of the impersonal, Universal One in an enlightened man. This term derives from classical Hinduism.

Bhagavad Gita.   A poetic epic originally written in Sanskrit. The *Bhagavad Gita* is based on a dialogue between the warrior Arjuna and Krishna. It teaches principle Hindu themes through poetic prose.

Bilocation.   The Russian term for clairvoyance. This term is sometimes used as a synonym for out-of-body experiences.

Biofeedback.   The employment of instruments for the purpose of monitoring brain waves, heart rate, muscle tension, etc. This holistic technique is designed to help people control these and other involuntary body processes.

Channeling.   The process of receiving information from either the "higher self" or a metaphysical entity. A channeler (modern term for a medium) is the human contact between the physical world and the ethereal dwelling of the spiritual entity. The channeler usually goes into a trance during the process of making contact with the spiritual being from the incorporeal world.

Chakras.   The seven energy centers of the human body. The kundalini must be generated through the chakras by means of meditation. When the kundalini reaches the crown chakra, at the top of the head, enlightenment results.

Clairaudience.   Extrasensory data perceived as sound by an individual.

Clairvoyance.   Extrasensory perception of physical objects or events. Clairvoyance is distinquished from ESP, which involves perception of thoughts.

Dissociation.   Separating the hemispheres of the mind so that each operates independently of the other.

Divination.   A method utilized for discovering personal significance relative to present or future events. The means of attaining this information may include dreams, mediumistic possession, consulting with the dead (necromancy), or "reading" natural phenomena.

Extrasensory Perception (ESP).   The experiencing of an external event, object, state, or influence while apparently transcending the physical senses.

Guru.   A spiritual teacher in the Hindu tradition who instructs his disciples in the way of enlightenment.

Holistic.   Refers to the wholeness of the individual as to his environment and the interdependence of his body, mind, and spirit. The term derives from the Greek *holos*, meaning "whole."

I Ching. A book of divination associated with Taoism.

Karma. The inexorable law of retributive justice derived from classical Hinduism. The bad karma accumulated in one's lifetime will determine one's status in the next life (i.e., reincarnation).

Kirilian. A type of photography allegedly designed to project the aura that emanates from plants, animals, and humans. The aura is subject to change, according to occultists, due to physiological or emotional changes.

Kinesiology. The study of the principles of anatomy relative to human movement.

Kundalini. An alleged psycho-spiritual power at the base of the spine, according to Yogis. Kundalini is known as "the serpent power."

Mantra. A holy word, phrase, or verse repeated several times in succession for the purpose of entrancement and a sense of union with the divine source within the individual. Mantras derive from Hindu or Buddhist meditation techniques.

Metaphysics. Beyond the physical; supernatural.

Monism. "All is One." All of reality is an undivided organism, a "seamless garment." Monism is often used in a philosophical context, while pantheism holds religious connotations.

Mysticism. God cannot be known or understood propositionally, but must be realized by a contentless mind. Spiritual union with Ultimate Reality is obtained through subjective intuitive experience according to mysticism.

Naturalism. A world view that denies the supernatural and seeks a natural explaination for the existence of the universe.

Neopaganism. Nature worshippers deriving from occult initiation rites. Witchcraft and ceremonial magic are a part of neopagan practices.

Nirvana. Used in Buddhism to refer to the final release from the cycle of reincarnation into bliss.

Numerology. Study of the occult significance of numbers through the use of divination.

Occult. Hidden or secret knowledge of the supernatural.

Pantheism. The world and God are of one essence. The belief that all is god and god is all. The world is then imbued with a consciousness. The god of pantheism is impersonal.

Paranormal. As related to psychic research, the paranormal refers to phenomena that is beyond the "normal."

Parapsychology. Also referred to as psychical research. Parapsychology investigates psi phenomena and communication. This field of psychology includes telepathy, ESP, and clairvoyance.

Precognition.　The prediction or knowledge of future events that cannot be inferred from present knowledge.

Premonition.　The anticipation of an event without conscious reason. Premonitions are usually ominous.

Psi.　The twenty-third letter of the Greek alphabet. Psi is the general term for extrasensory and extrasensorimotor activity. Psi includes telepathy, clairvoyance, precognition, and psychokinesis. The abbreviated term for psychic or parapsychological phenomena.

Psychic.　A synonym for sensitive or medium. The term psychic refers to the description of paranormal events and abilities that are inexplicable in terms of established physical principles.

Psychic Surgery.　A method of healing in which portions of diseased tissue are alledgedly removed without the use of medical instruments.

Psychokinesis.　PK or telekinesis. The direct influence of mind on matter (external physical process, condition, or object) without any known intermediate physical energy or instrumentation (involves the extramotor aspect of psi).

Psychometry.　Object reading or the paranormal ability of some sensitives to obtain facts about the history of an object, including people and events connected with it, usually through touching or handling it.

Reincarnation.　The belief that the soul passes from one bodily existence to the next following death. Following virtually innumerable inhabitations of bodily forms, the soul is eventually released to absorbtion in the Universal One.

Retrocognition.　Paranormal knowledge of past events beyond the range of inference from present evidence or memory on the part of the individual.

Samadhi.　According to classical Hinduism, this is enlightenment (God-consciousness). This term is synonymous with satori in Zen Buddhism.

Sorcery.　The use of magic and ritual for the purpose of manipulating natural and supernatural phenomena.

Synchronicity.　The alignment of the microcosm (man) with the macrocosm (environment), creating a sense of oneness.

Synergy.　The New Age concept of natural systems merging into holistic patterns. Synergy is effected through the sense of union between the macrocosm and the microcosm.

Syntropy.　A non-scientific theory that posits the self-organizing ability of living matter into increasingly complex patterns. This theory is in contradiction to the Second Law of Thermodynamics and the concept of entropy.

Tantra. Sacred scriptures in the Hindu and Buddhist tradition used for the purpose of immediate enlightenment. This term also refers to practices and techniques within these traditions.

Tao. A Chinese concept believed to govern the operations of the universe and known as the Way (pronounced "dow").

Tarot. Colorful picture cards used for divination or fortunetelling.

Telekinesis. A form of PK referring to the movement of stationary objects apart from the use of any known physical force.

Telepathy. ESP of another person's mental state or thoughts.

Trance. Gaining access to otherwise inhibited dimensions of the body-mind system through a self-induced state of altered consciousness.

Upanishads. This philosophical literature describes the nature of truth and ultimate reality. The Vedas are included in the last section of the Upanishads.

Vedas. Sacred Hindu texts that include a collection of hymns, poetry, ceremonies, advice for the retired, and teachings on monistic philosophy. Vedic Hinduism refers to the principal concepts of the Vedas.

Witchcraft. Black magic, sorcery, occultic practices, especially those related to casting spells and necromancy (spiritism; spiritualism; mediums). Wicca refers to a male magician from the Old English tradition. Also involves ritual magic and neopaganism.

Yoga. A means to enlightenment through the conditioning of the individual physically, psychically, and spiritually. Literally the term refers to "yoking" or "joining."

Yogi. A teacher of methods of yoga.

Zen. A two-branched strain of Buddhist thought that emphasizes an individual's detachment from logical and rational thought as a means to enlightenment.

Zodiac. Imaginary path of the planets (excepting Pluto) divided into twelve constellations. The Zodiac is founded upon the assumption that the sun enters each of several "houses" or symbols. The Zodiac is consulted for astrological predictions.

This glossary of terms was compiled from a variety of sources.